THE RACE TO BE MYSELF

CASTER
THE
RACE

SEMENYA

TO BE MYSELF

Norton Young Readers

An Imprint of W. W. Norton & Company
Independent Publishers Since 1923

For those who are born different and feel they don't belong in this world, it is because you were brought here to help create a new one.

For information about permission to reproduce selections from this book, write to
Permissions, W. W. Norton & Company, Inc., 500 Fifth Avenue, New York, NY 10110

For information about special discounts for bulk purchases, please contact
W. W. Norton Special Sales at specialsales@wwnorton.com or 800-233-4830

Manufacturing by Versa Press
Book design by Hana Anouk Nakamura
Production manager: Delaney Adams

ISBN 978-1-324-03097-3

W. W. Norton & Company, Inc., 500 Fifth Avenue, New York, N.Y. 10110
www.wwnorton.com

W. W. Norton & Company Ltd., 15 Carlisle Street, London W1D 3BS

1 2 3 4 5 6 7 8 9 0

CONTENTS

THE
RACE
TO BE
MYSELF

PROLOGUE

I AM MOKGADI CASTER SEMENYA. I AM ONE OF THE greatest track-and-field athletes to ever run the 800-meter distance (800 meters is two laps around a standard-sized track). I've won two Olympic gold medals and three world championships, among many other victories, and went unbeaten for almost four years. Unfortunately, it is not what I have achieved on the track that has likely brought me to your attention. Much has been written about me in major media around the world since I came into the public's eye in 2009, and most of it is lies or half-truths. I have waited a long time to tell my story. For more than a decade I have preferred to let my running do the talking. After what has happened to me, it felt easier that way.

In 2019, the International Association of Athletics Federation (or IAAF, now World Athletics) banned me from running my favored 800-meter event, along with the 400-meter and the 1,500-meter distances. I was not banned because I was caught using drugs to help my performance or cheating. Rather, I am no longer allowed to run those distances because of a biological condition I was born with and that I refuse to take unnecessary drugs to change.

I have what is called a difference of sex development (DSD), a genetic condition where an embryo (a fertilized egg in a mother that divides and becomes a human being) responds in a different way to the hormones produced during pregnancy. These hormonal changes affect the development of internal and external sexual organs. To put it simply, on the outside I am female and I have a vagina, but I do not have a uterus. I do not menstruate, and my body produces an elevated amount of testosterone, a reproductive hormone that gives me more typically masculine characteristics than other women, such as a deeper voice and fewer curves. I cannot carry a child because I don't have a uterus, but I do not produce sperm (the male egg that fertilizes a female's egg and creates an embryo). I did not know any of this about my body until soon after August 2009, when I won the gold medal in the 800-meter race at the world championships in Berlin. I was only eighteen years old and had been forced to undergo a humiliating medical procedure without my consent just prior to the race.

The scientific community has labeled my biological makeup as "intersex," and I am now one of the most, if not the most, recognizable intersex persons in the world. The truth is I don't think of myself that way. I want everyone to understand that even though I am built differently than other women, I am a woman. Of course, growing up I knew I looked and behaved differently from many of my peers, but my family, my community, and my country just understood I was what the Western world calls a "tomboy." They accepted me as I was and never made me feel like an outsider. This is the source of my strength. I have never questioned who I am.

And I know I am many things—a proud Black woman from Limpopo, a rural province in the northernmost part of South Africa, a daughter, a sister, a wife, and now I am a mother to two young girls. I feel and hurt just like a regular person, although I am not considered by science or some people to be a regular woman. And I am a runner. It is like meditating for me. Every time I get to the starting line of a race, my mind goes completely silent. I hear nothing except my own breathing. I see nothing except the track in front of me. Some people call this "the zone."

I sometimes remind myself of how blessed I am to be where I am today. Not that many years ago, the sports governing body of my own country of South Africa wouldn't have allowed me to run in the Olympics because I am Black. I was born in 1991, just a few years before the first democratic elections in 1994 would finally begin to unravel apartheid, the system of government that defined people and even ripped families apart based on the color of their skin and other physical features. (Under apartheid, people were labeled as "White," "Black," "Indian," or "Colored," meaning mixed race. Society was divided along these racial lines, and there were laws against people from one racial group mixing with or marrying people from another group.) My parents, older siblings, and extended family lived through this time. They were not allowed to travel or live where they wanted; some were forcibly relocated. Black people didn't have access to higher education. And unlike me, so many great Black athletes never got a chance. There is still so much trauma in our communities from the brutality of apartheid. I carry within me that history of discrimination and resistance and the yearning for freedom; they are there in everything I do.

As a young girl, I heard Nelson Mandela, the beloved leader of our country and icon of freedom and resistance around the world, speak about sports as having "the power to inspire . . . the power to unite people in a way that little else does . . ." And I loved sports. I knew from a young age that I wanted to be known and appreciated for my physical talents. No notable athletes had ever come out of our small village, and people were more concerned with surviving than dreaming. I had no real reason to believe in my eventual success, but I was sure I was going to make it.

I was lucky to be born with these special talents—my mind has a unique ability to focus, my body can stand the pain and exhaustion of endless training. It's not the testosterone in my body that makes me great, it's my ambition, perseverance, and faith in myself. Every time I've been knocked down, I get back up. Every setback has made me stronger.

I have never spoken in detail about what happened in Berlin on August 19, 2009, when my gender was first questioned by the sports authorities and my life was forever changed, but I am now ready to do so. It is said that silence will not protect us. I have been vilified and persecuted. Journalists have descended into my village and every school I'd ever attended. My parents and siblings, friends, and teachers have been harassed with calls and by visitors, day and night. I can still hear my mother wailing desperately as she tried to explain to perfect strangers that I was born a girl, and that I was her little girl, and why was all of this happening? "I don't have time for nonsense," I have replied to the journalists who've approached me about the "gender issue" throughout the years. And I mean it. Because that's how I've always seen it. Nonsense and stupidity and ignorance. I'm here to run.

All I have endured has affected me in ways I cannot describe, although I will try. And while I have faced significant hardships throughout my life, I want to make clear that my story is not one of pain and torment, but rather about hope, self-confidence, and resilience. I am still standing; I am still here.

I am not a scientist. I am not here to deliver a lecture on human biology. I am not here to prove my humanity—*that* has been granted to me by God. I accept and love myself just the way I am. I am fortunate to have a family who never tried to change me, and a country that wrapped its arms around me and fought for my right to run. There is always a sadness to endings, but I will run as long as my body allows me to. When I can no longer run, you will still see me on the track supporting the coming generations.

I am a proud South African woman born in a tiny village to people who loved me. They have survived more humiliations than I could possibly know. It is from them that I know about maintaining dignity in the face of oppression. It is my hope that by telling my truth, I inspire others to be unafraid, to love and accept themselves. May this story contribute to a more tolerant world for us all.

CHAPTER ONE
GOD MADE ME

I'M RUNNING HARD AND FAST. THE GROUND HAS cracks everywhere, and I keep tripping. I am climbing over metal fences and floating and then falling and pushing up with my body and floating again. My feet are caked with dirt, and they are also wet. Sometimes they hurt, but the pain goes away. I am happy. No one can catch me. My mother and sisters try, but I'm too fast for them. I believe this is the first time I felt like "me." That I was a person, separate from the people and things around me. It is my earliest memory. I was around two years old.

My mother says I was an early walker. I took my first steps at seven months. From there, it seemed like I was flying from one place to the next. My feet were always bleeding because the floor of my parents' home was made of rough cement. It was easy for a toddler to stumble and fall, and my legs and knees were always scratched and bruised. They said I wouldn't cry when I fell, I'd just get up and keep going. And I was strong. If my older siblings wanted to take something away from me, they'd have to work hard to pry it out of my tiny hands. Even as a toddler,

Me at six months old in Ga-Masehlong.
I would start walking the following month.

I was fierce. My mom said she knew I was something special right from the start.

I was born to Dorcas and Jacob Semenya on January 7, 1991, in a village called Ga-Masehlong, located in what is today called Limpopo, the northernmost province of South Africa. Our village is small and remote; only about a thousand people lived there. There was a time when it couldn't be found on Google Maps. There is only one road that leads into the village. If you were driving from the city of Polokwane, capital of the Limpopo province, you'd drive about 60 kilometers (about 37 miles) northwest on the only main road, and then make a left and head into nothing but open sky, wilderness, and dirt tracks. Eventually you would arrive at a tree that holds a sign with our village's name on it.

We had eight main streets. Mostly there were homes on rectangular plots of land and a few shops, what we call "spaza" or "tuck" shops, convenience stores that sell basic household items and snacks and drinks. Anyone could put up a spaza shop; many were in people's homes. We had one liquor store, a supermarket, and a primary school. And, of course, we had a church. You'd find almost everybody gathered there on Sundays, and sometimes during the week, singing, dancing, and calling out to God and his Son. Many people left during the day to work as farmers and laborers and domestic workers in towns and cities or in the larger neighboring villages.

I've often described my village as "a dusty, dusty place." And it was that. The flat, dry land surrounding the homes seemed like it could go on forever. It was dotted with baobab and jacaranda trees, bushes, brambles, and thorns. You could see mountains in the distance. When I was growing up, the houses were made of mud and stone. Some folks built their roofs with tin, and others used tightly woven dried grass or thatch. There was wire fencing around many of the homes to keep in the cows and goats and sheep, although the animals would also roam freely around the village. Everyone in the village knew each other, and kids were allowed to roam freely, too. We call the wilderness surrounding our village "the bush," and it's where I spent most of my childhood.

My mom had been a teacher in her youth, but once she married my father, he preferred that she stay home. My mom still wanted to contribute financially to our family, so she opened a spaza shop in our yard. She sold mostly foods like raw cuts of meat and fish and sweets. During the week, she would also take some merchandise to our school and sell to students during lunch breaks, like candy and fresh-baked bread with raisins. My mother was beautiful, with rich brown skin and a rounded face and curves. Like most of the women in my family, she was not tall, but she carried herself with a dignity that made her seem much taller. My mom was very motherly, by which I mean patient, kind,

1995. My mom and dad's wedding. Third outfit change.

and protective. I inherited her easy, wide smile. She was tough, too—not a woman you wanted to cross.

My father worked as a gardener in Pretoria, a city about 310 kilometers (192 miles) from our village. The work kept him away from home a lot, sometimes for months at a time.

I loved my mom with all my heart, but I was what they call a "daddy's girl." I missed him terribly when he would go off to the big city. I remember he would come home and I would run to him and hug him for a long time. He'd pick me up and spin me around and around. Most would say I inherited my height and facial features from my father, who was thin and long limbed but muscular, with sharp cheekbones. He, too, had a big smile. My dad could come off as shy and reserved, but he also loved to joke, and it seemed you could hear his laughter from miles away.

I am the fourth child of six children, five girls and one boy. My eldest sister, Wenny, was born in 1980, and then Nico was born in 1985, followed by Olga, born in 1987. I came into the world in 1991, and my younger sister Murriel was born in 1993. My baby brother, Ishmael, the only boy in our family and the final child, was born in 1996. The real baby of our family was my niece, Neo, Wenny's daughter, who lived with us from the day she was born in 1998. My older sisters would come and go from the village as they searched for opportunities in schooling and work in Johannesburg, the largest city in South Africa. When they left, I would be the eldest in the household, and the main caretaker of my younger sister, brother, and niece while my mother and father worked. I had plenty of extended family in our village—aunts and uncles on both sides with children of their own.

1970s. My father at work gardening in Pretoria in protective equipment.

We were not rich people, but we were not poor. Our family may not have had a lot, but we had plenty of food. I never had to go to bed hungry. For me, being poor is when a family doesn't have clothes, and they don't know where their next meal is coming from. "Poor" is when you don't have shelter. Our family had all of this, so we weren't poor.

Our home was large by our standards, with five bedrooms and a living room. We were a big family, and we needed the space. There was no electricity or running water. We fetched enough water from the village well for our needs and used candles and oil lamps. When I was four or five years old, my father installed a solar energy system; government-run electricity didn't come to our village until 2001, when I was ten. Our toilet was outdoors, a good walk away from the main house. It was a wooden shack built around a deep hole in the ground. We called it "the long drop." No need for water to flush. You sat and did your business and went on with life.

On our small piece of land, we grew fruits and vegetables (including lemons, oranges, figs, guava, mangoes, peaches, grapes, pomegranates, sugarcane, tomatoes, potatoes, and spinach) on one side and kept our animals on the other. We didn't sell what we grew; we farmed only to feed ourselves. There was an area inside the house that could be called a kitchen, but the actual cooking of meals happened outside in our yard. I loved to run into the bush and collect firewood. We had a pit in the back of our home, and when the wood was glowing red and orange, we'd put our iron pots on it. We owned about thirty domesticated animals—cows and goats and sheep. I loved to take care of them, too.

My mother told me one of our ancestors came to her in a dream while she was pregnant and gave her my full name. Mokgadi Caster Semenya. Mokgadi was my maternal grandmother's name. In Pedi, our native tongue, it means "one who guides" and "one who gives up what they want so that others may have what they need." Caster is an English name, and I learned it means "one who seeks."

I weighed twelve pounds at birth, the biggest of all my siblings. I was barrel chested, my mother said, with big lungs that allowed for a deep-throated cry, unlike any of her other daughters. I know that after three girls, my parents probably wanted a boy, but here I was. They were happy. A new healthy soul in the family is always a cause for happiness.

My parents adored me. If they did have a favorite child, it would have been me. I kept going back to that feeling of being loved by the two most important people in my life when later it seemed the rest of the world thought I was some kind of monster.

CHAPTER TWO

A DIFFERENT KIND OF GIRL

AS I GREW OLDER, IT BECAME CLEAR I WASN'T interested in the same things other girls were. I'd be given a doll or teddy bear, and I would toss it around a bit and then get rid of it. I also didn't want to play make-believe or hand-clapping games with the other girls. I wasn't affectionate, and I didn't want to be kissed or held much. What I wanted was to run around, take things apart and figure out how they worked, and I didn't care about getting dirty or hurt.

I remember the day my father came home after one of his long stays in Pretoria. He would usually bring us gifts and other household necessities. This time, he was holding up a dress for me. It was red and white and it had ruffles and lace around the hem with a little belt that tied around the waist.

"Mokgadi, my baby, this is a nice one," my father said with a big smile on his face while turning the dress this way and that.

"Thank you, Daddy. It's nice. It's a fine dress. But I don't want to wear it."

"Why not?" My father acted surprised but I know he wasn't.

"I will not wear it. I don't like it."

"Maybe you try it on first and then you see what you think." My father pretended to be sad with an exaggerated frown on his face.

"No. You wear it first. You should lead by example, like you say to me. See how it suits you. If you like wearing it, then I'll wear it." It was playful talk between us but it was how I really felt.

Instead of forcing me to wear it or calling my mother for help, I remember my father just shook his head, laughed, and said, "OK, Mokgadi. As you wish."

That was the day I stopped wearing dresses. I was maybe five or six years old.

Dresses and skirts didn't suit the life I was leading. I spent my days fetching firewood and pails of water from the village well. I loved going around our yard and tending to our fruits and vegetables. By then I'd even started heading into the bush with my older cousins to learn how to care for our animals. The bush had all kinds of things that could hurt you. At least wearing pants gave you a fighting chance against something like a sneaky cobra. And I played soccer with the boys in my village. There's a lot of falling and jostling in soccer. I needed more protection than dresses offered.

My parents were true believers; they had a deep faith in God and made sure their children had the same. We went to the church in the middle of our village every Sunday. People would gather outdoors and sit on these white plastic chairs. I loved the singing and dancing and clapping. The service would last for hours with several pastors delivering hour-long sermons one after the other.

Everyone clean and nicely dressed and ready to hear the word of the Lord. The women wore skirts and dresses. But I decided I wasn't going to do that anymore. One Sunday I came out of my room wearing a freshly laundered and ironed pair of pants and button-down shirt I'd gotten from one of my cousins. My mother saw me and didn't say a word. It was expected for girls and women to wear dresses and skirts and men to wear pants and button shirts, at least in church. But there weren't actual rules about it.

Looking back, I'm sure there were comments from nosy adults, but my parents shielded me from those. If anything, as I got older, my mother and father would show appreciation for the things I was willing to do in the household. They'd marvel at how strong and fearless I was and tell me I was a child of God.

We may have accepted Christianity, but we still believed in our gods, our ancestors, and our African traditions. We often combined the two. Our ancestors didn't make regulations about girls not being able to wear pants when they wanted, so what could a pastor in my village complain about, really?

Our church had a boys' choir and a girls' choir, and they took turns singing to the congregation. They never sang together, always separate. I loved to hear the boys singing. The girls were good, but I preferred the boys' voices. They sounded more like me. This one day, I guess I was filled with the spirit because I jumped up and ran over and started dancing and singing with the boys. No one stopped me. There was no rule that said girls couldn't sing with boys. People seemed to think what I did was funny because they laughed and clapped along to the beat.

In my part of the world, the issue of gender is simple. If you are born with a vagina, then you are a girl. Hanging around with boys, dressing like them or playing sports with them, didn't change that. Occasionally I was mistaken for a boy, but I wasn't offended and people didn't argue or insult me. Most of the time they apologized and that was that. I was never made to feel like anything was wrong with my behaving differently from other girls. And I wasn't the only girl who was "boyish" in my village. Girls who preferred to wear trousers or who played with boys weren't considered abominations. There are many ways to be a girl.

I did have some run-ins with bullies, mostly boys. Kids can be cruel. But I learned from a young age how to deal with them.

"Hey Mokgadi . . . you look like a boy."

"I know I look like a boy. What are you going to do about it?"

"Why don't you put a dress on and go play with girls?"

"I don't think I'm going to do that. So, like I said, what are you going to do about it?"

By that point I and this unfortunate kid, whoever he was, would be standing eye to eye, because I was a pretty tall girl. The other kids already would have swarmed around us, anticipating a show. I didn't like wasting time when it came to these arguments. I had things to do and places to be. I let my fists finish the conversation, and soon the bully would find himself knocked back on the ground. I know that violence is never the answer, and I wouldn't necessarily teach my daughters to throw the first punch. My wife and I plan to teach our daughters to resolve things with words, to walk away from nonsense. That is, unless someone puts their hands on them. Now that's a different story. But when I was growing up, if you disrespected me, well . . . you were going to feel it one way or the other. That's the law of the bush.

In Ga-Masehlong, I had to be tough, show the boys I wasn't to be made fun of. I'm not particularly proud of the beatings I handed out, but I never started a fight with anyone. If someone started with me, I knew how to finish it good. Once I knocked down whatever boy was making fun of me, you could see their brains calculating what to do next—the options were to get up and fight and risk the embarrassment of what could be a severe beating from a girl, or . . . maybe it was wiser to have me on their side. Most of the time they chose wisely.

"Eh, Mokgadi," they'd say while wiping the dust off their pants. "Come on now. I was just playing with you. No need for all this. Heard you were a good striker. Let's go kick."

The bullies became competitors or teammates, all of us running barefoot on the dusty soccer pitches of our village. They learned to respect me because I respected myself. I was fair, I minded my business, and I could play well. I'm still friends with many of those boys today, all now men with families of their own.

All of my sisters took after my mom—they were short, very curvy and pretty, while I was tall, with a wiry muscular frame. They'd wear skirts and dresses and form-hugging clothing, while I preferred my clothes to be loose. I liked that American street style of baggy jeans and shirts.

I loved my siblings. But there were definitely times when we would get on each other's nerves. We only had one television in our house, and when my sisters were home, they always wanted to watch stupid romantic movies. I wanted to watch things that were exciting— action movies, sports, stuff like that. So we'd fight over the channel. Each of us would get up and change the channel or stand in front of the TV to prevent the other one from changing it. Of course, during those fights, they'd talk about my clothing.

"Mokgadi, what are you wearing those clothes for? You're really starting to look like a boy now."

And my answer to them was the same throughout the years: "So what?"

Eventually I was the only one who could fix the TV when it broke. I realized all I had to do was make sure it didn't work when my sisters wanted to watch those silly movies. Then they'd go do something else and I'd get it working again so I could watch what I wanted.

The thing that really pricked my sisters' skin, though, was the household chores.

Where I come from, everyone must contribute to the maintenance of the household, even small children. As I grew bigger and stronger, I made it known that I didn't want to do things like cooking or cleaning. I wanted to do things that challenged me physically, like gardening and taking care of the animals. Of course, it doesn't work that way. As a child, especially a girl child, you are supposed to do what you are told. My sisters would constantly remind me of this.

"Mokgadi. It's your turn to wash the dishes," my older sister Nico would say.

And I'd suck my teeth. "NO. I told you already, *I* don't wash dishes. *You* wash dishes."

One thing I can say about my older sisters is that I was much more afraid of them than any bully in the village. When I refused to do as Nico said, she would have no choice but to give me a few good slaps to keep me in line. But my sister would have to catch me first. I'd mouth off, and then when I saw she'd had enough and was getting ready to put her hands on me, I'd take off running. Sometimes I'd make Nico run to the end of the village and back again.

People would see me barreling down the road and jump

out of the way. They knew what was going on. Nico had been a good middle-distance runner in her school days, but she could never catch me. At least not until I was ready to be caught. When her legs were gone and she was bent over gasping for air, I'd stop and come back to her.

"Are you done, sister? Are you OK? What was the point of the chase, Nico? You know you'll never catch me," I'd say while patting her back and smiling and waiting for her to catch her breath. Then we'd walk or jog back to our house, laughing about everything, and we'd wash the dishes together.

CHAPTER THREE
I AM NOT AFRAID

OUR SCHOOL BUILDINGS WERE SIMPLE, SQUARE-shaped cement structures. The classrooms were orderly; each had wooden desks for the students, the teacher's desk, and one large chalkboard at the front. The students were responsible for keeping the classrooms clean. We'd all sweep and mop and dust every inch of the rooms on a schedule.

Aside from subjects like reading and writing and basic math, the girls—and only the girls—had to learn what was called "handwork," which was stuff like sewing and knitting. It didn't make sense to me. What did I need to learn to sew for? I remember being annoyed and doing just enough in this class to get by. My guy friends got to do the gardening outdoors, and they'd occasionally come to the classroom window and point and laugh at me because they knew how much I hated it.

There weren't any sports facilities—no basketball courts,

Classmates and me on classroom cleaning day.

no gyms, no running track or manicured soccer fields. We had a large outdoor space, dusty ground strewn with grass and sharp rocks here and there, surrounded by wire fencing to keep the kids inside. I'd play soccer there with the boys.

Once the lunch break was over, the kids would head back to class, but not me. I'd try to find a way to sneak back home. School felt like a cage compared to the freedom I enjoyed at home. My mother got so tired of me skipping out on classes and getting notices from my teachers that she finally had no choice but to call in the Village Granny.

The Village Granny is one of those IYKYK things. She's probably not your blood grandmother, but she feels like everyone's grandmother. More importantly, all the kids respected her. She was that woman in the community who walks around as if she's part police officer and part witch. Fear is the Village Granny's superpower.

Well, our Village Granny had never come across someone like me.

"Get her," I told my mother. "I'm not afraid of that woman."

The Village Granny showed up in our yard. The old woman was a formidable figure. Tall and strong looking. She was old, yes, but not frail. She could hurt someone if she wanted to. I could see she was a person I should respect, but I did not feel any fear.

And then she spoke.

"Mokgadi. Go to school. *Right now.* Or I will punish you." Her voice sounded like mine, deep and powerful. I was taller than any other girl in my village, but this Village Granny was even taller than me. Much taller than my mom, too.

I held my ground. This woman was standing in *my* yard,

trying to tell me what to do. I placed my hands on my hips and lifted my chin.

"No. If you want someone to go to school, take your own grandchildren."

I remember that woman looked at me as if I were a demon. Nobody talked to her like that. For a second it seemed like she didn't know what to do, but then she gathered herself.

"You're wasting your time, Granny. I'm not scared of you." Then I turned toward the bush that surrounded us. I swept my arm around as if showcasing our landscape, the wild grasses fading off in the horizon toward the mountains. "You better be a good runner."

I knew that no old woman, no matter how strong looking, was going to follow me into that, so I continued, "*I* will go to school when *I* want to."

And right when Granny tried to grab me, I took off running. I wasn't scared of anyone. Not even her.

My teachers would complain to my mom. I didn't dedicate myself to my schoolwork the way the other kids did. If there was a shortcut to my studies, I'd find it. I wasn't a bad kid. I just didn't want to take the extra time required to excel in schoolwork. My priorities were playing sports and hanging out. Of course, this was upsetting to my parents, who valued education above all else because they grew up during apartheid, and they'd never gotten the opportunity to study in the way we did.

When you're young, you feel invincible. I trusted in my body. I spent my time after chores climbing trees, chasing after wild animals. Jumping off cliffs with my cousins into roaring rivers. I wouldn't say we were swimming, exactly, but we knew how to survive in the water. We used empty soda bottles with the tops screwed on tightly to stay afloat. I'd earned my place among those boys. I could do anything they could do.

One day, though, I found out this incredible body of mine had its limitations.

We needed bread, and word was out in the village that there was a good batch just baked at a spaza shop a little ways from us. My older sister Olga and I went off together and, as often happened, we started racing. Olga was keeping up with me, but there was a corner coming up. I knew if I took it at full speed, I'd leave her in the dust. Normally people slow down at bends, but not me. I wasn't afraid to run around the corner as fast as my seven-year-old legs could go. I might've even picked up speed as I made the turn. The next thing I remember was a click in my right knee. I kept running but I knew something wasn't right.

Olga and I got the bread and then we walked back home. My leg felt off but I didn't complain, and there wasn't any pain. When we got home, I went to the room I shared with my sister and lay down. Now the leg was hurting. I must've fallen asleep because the next thing I remember is my mother waking me up and asking me what was wrong.

I told her I hurt my leg, and when I showed her, my knee was almost three times its normal size.

"My Lord! Mokgadi." My mother looked horrified. "What happened?"

I told my mom that something clicked in my knee when I was running with Olga to buy the bread, but my mom didn't believe me.

"Climbing a tree. You must've fallen from a tree, tell me the truth!" She was concerned for my leg, but I could hear the change in my mother's tone. She was getting angry.

"You never listen to me. Playing with those boys. You're going to kill yourself one day. Look at you now, Mokgadi. Look at this leg of yours," she said, shaking her head.

"I'm telling you I wasn't with the boys. I was running with Olga to get the bread."

My sister was scared and tried to testify on my behalf, but my mom wouldn't listen.

"Be quiet, Olga. You're covering for her." When my mom got mad, there was no getting through to her.

Eventually it didn't matter how I hurt myself because the following day the leg was even bigger and I couldn't move it at all. And now I was in serious pain. My mom took me to WF Knobel Hospital, where I'd been born seven years prior. We didn't have a car, so we had to wait and secure transport by minibus.

WF Knobel was part of South Africa's public health care system and was free of charge for all citizens. The hospital was clean and orderly, and it had a good reputation. The nurses, whom we called "sisters," didn't seem to know what to do at first. I remember how worried my mom looked. She'd been angry before, but now it broke her heart she couldn't do anything more for me.

"You're strong, my girl. You're so strong. You'll be OK," she said, and stroked my hair and cheeks.

I was in so much pain; I just buried my face in her neck. At some point they were able to take X-rays and told us it looked like I'd dislocated my right kneecap. I'd taken the corner so fast my kneecap had basically popped out of where it lived. They couldn't put it back, so I was admitted to the hospital and given a bed until they figured things out.

Eventually the doctors decided I needed to have surgery. There was no other way to fix me. My people have some distrust of Western medical practices; we mainly believed in traditional ways of healing with herbs and prayer. But at this point my parents understood the traditional ways weren't going to help, and that surgery was the only option for me to ever walk properly again. Unfortunately, our public health care system was what it was. I had to wait for a specialist who could do the operation, and I would remain in the hospital for almost seven months before one became available.

Seven months of my life in a hospital room. Looking back, it's difficult to believe it. A wild girl like me, used to roaming free in her village and playing in the bush every day, was trapped in a hospital for seven months. I missed my family and cousins and friends. I even missed my teachers.

I said I had a happy childhood—this event is the only bad thing I can remember. Not one for tears, I would cry my eyes out when my parents and siblings would visit me. When they could, they'd bring me fruits and sweets, or buy me ice cream. They would try to cheer me up and tell me about whatever was going on in the village. But all I wanted was to go home. There were days I would jump off the bed when their visit was over and hobble after them. I was so desperate to be with my family, I'd have to be physically restrained by the sisters.

Finally, my family was told they'd found a surgeon who could operate and I was transferred to a different hospital. My mother came with me and spent the night. I was back at WF Knobel the day after my surgery, and then I was discharged after about a week. I'd gone into the hospital in early March, and I came home in September. Part of me would miss the constant attention and the kindness of the sisters, but I was happy to be out of my prison.

This injury could've ended any chance I ever had to be a professional athlete. Most people don't know this injury has bothered me my entire career. Today, my right leg is weaker than my left leg. Since the day I was released from the hospital to this very day, I have a very distinct walk. I wouldn't say I'm limping, exactly, but it's different. The leg never healed properly. We weren't given any advice about what kinds of exercises would strengthen my leg after the surgery. There was no follow-up physical therapy for this village girl. I went home and resumed my life. I started playing soccer again and running around with my friends. Sometimes, just for fun, I like to think about how much I've accomplished with this injured right leg and how much more I could've won if I'd had two good ones.

CHAPTER FOUR
PLAYING WITH BOYS

BY THE TIME I WAS FOUR YEARS OLD, I HAD STARTED kicking around balls with my male cousins and the other neighborhood kids. There'd be some girls who would play with us, too, but it was mostly boys. Our people were obsessed with soccer, though we called it football. We didn't have an actual soccer ball, but we would kick around whatever we had—empty bottles, or we'd make balls out of pieces of cloth and plastic shopping bags.

When I was around eight years old, whenever I'd see an airplane, I would point up to the sky and tell my sisters, "One day, it'll be me on that plane you see up there. And I'll be passing over this village. Yes . . . I'll be on my way to somewhere big. Everyone will know my name."

My sisters would roll their eyes and say my brains were messed up. They didn't understand where I came up with these things. Only rich people traveled the world. But for me, it was as good as a done deal. Almost like a vision.

"You'll see. I'm telling you. One day, I will be the one who carries this household." Even though I didn't see any girls playing soccer on the TV we had just bought, I was so good I dreamt the men would have to let me play on the national teams.

My father always encouraged my soccer-playing dreams. He loved the way I handled the ball. "Heh! Heh! Did you see my daughter out there? How many goals did she hit this time?" I'd hear him brag to his friends when he was home.

When my dad was around, we loved to talk about strategy and moves and watch games together. Sometimes my dad would help me with my grips and tackles. He knew I was playing with the boys and had to be careful—I had to earn their respect on the field.

But I knew I could handle their heat. The boys were rough and I was rough, too. In fact, I played better than most of them. I was a versatile player: I could be a striker or a defender. I knew how to handle the ball, how to open space on the pitch, how to dribble. No one cared I was a girl, they just wanted to win. The kids and adults would all gather to see me play and they'd chant "Mokgadi! Mokgadi! Mokgadi!" I loved to hear my name. I loved to give a show to those who came to see me.

Eventually it got so people would bet on whatever game I was in. One thing about the village: we may not have had a lot of money, but people could find a few rand (the official currency of South Africa) for betting. Even kids would practice betting with biscuits and candies.

By the time I was ten, I was playing with boys older than me. Imagine a ten-year-old girl on a pitch with fourteen- and fifteen-year-old boys. Soccer is a rough game. Things could get dangerous, but I wasn't afraid. I remember we were playing a practice game on a Saturday afternoon. It was one of those days when everything I tried was going my way. My own teammate didn't like it. I don't know if he was jealous of the way I handled the ball or what. We'd never had any problems before but we weren't friends. He was just a guy on the team. He played well and I didn't really care about him one way or the other.

I was playing barefoot. His family could afford soccer cleats. At some point during the game, he stepped on top of my right foot. It wasn't a mistake; that I knew. My foot immediately swelled and I had to limp off the field. I went home angry. But there was an unspoken understanding between me and my teammates. I wasn't going to make a big deal of it and mess up the game.

My foot was so messed up I couldn't hunt in the bush or take out our animals. It took me about a month to get back on the field. When I returned to the team, this kid looked scared to death. He was older than me but knew what kind of person and player I was. If you purposefully tried to hurt me, I was going to make you pay for that.

The thing was this—after a month away from the field I had a lot of time to think about the incident. I decided to let it go. I was getting older, less impulsive. On that team I was a defender and he was a striker. If I decided to destroy his leg, he wouldn't have been out for just a month—this kid would never make it back to any soccer match. He was a good player; it was in the best interest of the team that he stay on.

"Hey! Mokgadi!" he yelled when he saw me. He ran over before I could walk to the rest of the group.

"Sorry about what happened. It was my fault. Things ran away from me. We missed you out here. Happy you're back," he said, and he did look sorry. More like terrified.

"Yo. Whatever. Let's play," I said as I walked away.

Soccer is like that. It can be a cruel game. People got emotional in this game we loved. Especially when there were biscuits and rand involved. The important thing I was starting to learn here was how to stay calm, how to keep my anger under control. I needed to understand that the game itself was more important than just me.

CHAPTER FIVE
THE CHANGE

IN THE BEGINNING, THE BOYS AND GIRLS IN MY VILLAGE within my age group looked the same. Then at a certain age some fundamental bits began to change. The boys grew taller, they grew hair on their faces and other places, and their voices changed. The girls would also sprout hair in new places, their chests would blossom into breasts and their hips would widen, and eventually they would begin to menstruate.

Obviously, being that I was a girl, I thought the changes I saw in these girls and that I had seen in my sisters would happen to me, too. Except nothing was happening for me. But I wasn't worried about it. I wasn't in a rush to develop breasts and get my period. I was playing sports, farming, taking care of our animals, and hunting. I figured having a period would get in the way because I saw how it got in the way of my sisters' and friends' lives. Sanitary pads and liners

2007. I'm sixteen years old. Class trip to a beach in Durban, swimming with my classmates and teachers.

weren't easy to get in Ga-Masehlong or even affordable for most of us. Girls in my village used whatever they could to contain the blood—old socks, rags, even notebook paper. I heard my sisters and friends complaining of pain and bloating. Truth is this thing sounded horrible. I started to feel like maybe not getting a period would be a gift.

I may not have been developing breasts, but eventually I began changing, too. My already deep voice got a little bit deeper; I grew even taller and more muscular. At this point it seemed normal. I wasn't built like my sisters to begin with. Anyone who spent every single day—boy or girl—playing soccer, boxing, running, and hunting was going to get strong. I was deeply aware of and loved my body. It was sturdy, agile, and flexible; I easily learned new moves and tricks. I could ask anything of my body and it would come through for me. I was happy the way I was, but I did wonder.

I decided to talk to the person I trusted more than anyone.

"Hey Mom, I don't think I'm going to get this period thing like the other girls."

"Why do you think this?" My mother turned and looked at me, her eyes wide, her voice serious and almost a whisper.

"I'm not getting breasts like them. I don't know, maybe it's just not going to happen for me."

My mom reassured me everything would be OK.

"You can't control nature. The only thing you can do is love yourself the way you are. God works in his own time, my child. Be grateful for the life you have been given."

Time went on. Every now and then I wondered why my sisters and friends had their boobs and I didn't have mine. Sometimes I'd stand naked in the mirror, turning this way and that, looking at my body from different angles, and I'd imagine what I'd look like if I did have them. Then I would just remind myself, This is the way things are supposed to be. Don't question God's will.

I hear that in the Western world, a girl like me would have been diagnosed and "treated" from birth or at least when puberty began. This didn't happen to me because no one thought there was anything to treat. We noticed I was

2007. School outing to South Beach, Durban. I took our teacher Mmamabolo's wig and posed as Tito Jackson. She still has no idea who took her wig. She'll know now when she reads the book.

"Spring lessons" at camp. Wearing provincial colors. Preparing for Commonwealth Youth Games in India.

different, but different didn't mean wrong. Some girls are what they call late bloomers, anyway.

My body may not have been changing in the way the other girls' were, but I felt something was happening to my brain. I became aware of feelings I hadn't dealt with before. I was comfortable being around boys. I understood their language and they understood mine. With girls, things were not exactly that way. When I tried hanging out with girls, they'd be talking about boys, which guy they thought was cute and who they wanted to kiss.

I wasn't interested in kissing any of the guys I was hanging out with. So when the girls got going on this kind of talk, which was often, I'd just walk away.

I don't want it to seem like I didn't have any friends who were girls, because I did, just not too many. I felt a little strange when I was around them, and I didn't know what that meant at the time. Girls could be bullies, too, and I remember more than a few would make fun of me. They'd talk about my secondhand clothes, my unkempt hair, my boyish-looking face. They'd make fun of me for being late to class or when I didn't understand a lesson. The girls' teasing did bother me, but in a different way than it did when boys did it. For starters, I didn't want to beat them up. If some girl got going with me, I'd just suck my teeth and simply say, "Look, girl, go away."

Later, it dawned on me that I didn't want to hit girls because I actually wanted to kiss them.

I think I first knew when I was about five years old, but at that age you don't really understand that it's a romantic feeling, just more of a curiosity. Once I got older and knew what was going on with me, I had to tell the most important people in my life.

One morning I told my family I had some news to share. It was one of those rare days when everybody was home. Even my dad. They all gathered in the living room.

"Look, don't expect me to come home with a boyfriend

because it will never happen. When I grow up, I'm going to marry a woman."

My family shook their heads, and there were some groans and eye-rolling and definitely some laughter. Just the usual stuff that meant: Here this crazy girl goes again talking some madness.

I don't know if they took me seriously that day, but there were no comments about it being "evil" or against our religion. No one in my family started screaming or crying. My parents and siblings did not seem surprised. They knew I was my own kind of person.

I was beginning to understand myself. What I wanted from life. I had my family, my friends, and soccer. I could have been a better student, but studying wasn't my focus. And then, as they say, all good things must come to an end. The life I'd built would change drastically one evening. I had just turned twelve years old.

"Mokgadi. Come here and talk to us," my father said when I walked in the door late one night. My parents looked serious, so I sat down and waited.

"Your grandmother in Fairlie is very old now. She is living with your cousins. They are boys. She needs help. We have decided you will live with her. It will be good for you. A new place," my mom said.

There was no arguing when your elders made such a decision for you. In our culture, it was normal to send one or more of your children to live at another family member's home. My sisters before me had been sent to various relatives' homes to help them with chores or child-rearing. I knew my turn would come, but I couldn't help but feel that my parents just wanted to get rid of me.

I was not an easy kid. My parents loved and accepted me, but no parent would be happy about their young daughter hanging out in the bush until late at night. I was wild, but I just didn't understand why they would want me to leave.

My heart was sore, but the village of Fairlie wasn't too far from my home. I could walk there in one hour or I could run there in half the time. I also believe my mother and father felt I was heading toward womanhood and perhaps it would be best for me to have a change of environment. I was too comfortable where I was. I ate, slept, played soccer, gambled, went to school only when I felt like it, and that was it. I was in the sixth grade there. They knew I was young enough to adapt, to grow, in a new place.

They were sending me to live with my grandmother because she needed a girl child to do traditional girl things. And this is what worried me. I was not a girl who did girl things. Everyone knew that. I knew my life would be completely different in her home. People loved and understood me in Ga-Masehlong. I would have to leave everything I knew, everything I'd built, and start all over again.

CHAPTER SIX
THABISO

THE DAY BEFORE I WAS TO LEAVE FOR FAIRLIE, MY mother packed my things. They included skirts, dresses, and blouses, and not one of the boys' items I was used to wearing. We didn't talk about it, but I understood. I could do and dress as I pleased in my birth village, but this girl was now heading to a new place. My mother knew I would eventually go back to wearing boy clothes, but I would have to toe the line as it was drawn when it came to such things and then find my way again.

I arrived in Fairlie early in January of 2003. I had turned twelve a day or so prior. My mother and I took a bus that morning. It was a short, quiet ride—maybe fifteen or twenty minutes—but it felt longer as we drove slowly on the rocky path and paused for the cows and goats that roamed freely and took their time crossing the road.

My grandmother met us at the door; she greeted me with joy.

"Welcome! Welcome, my grandchild. We are so happy! Happy to have Mokgadi here with us!" she said as she wrapped me in her thin arms and reached up and kissed my cheeks.

I remember her white dress and brightly colored head covering. She had my father's deep brown skin tone and the same warm eyes and big smile that showed her pink gums.

My grandmother's name was Mmaphuti Sekgala. She was what is known as a *ngaka*, a traditional healer. She was well known and respected for her ability to cure people of ailments using herbs and plants in the old ways of our ancestors. The sick and injured trusted her and came to her, even from neighboring villages. I would find out much later that she was actually my father's aunt and not his mother; not that such things made any difference. Her three grandsons lived with her—Kgabo, an adult whom I'd met before; Salvation, who was two years older than me; and Ernest, who was one year younger. This would be my first time meeting my two youngest cousins. We'd be going to school together and I'd have to rely on them to meet new people.

My grandmother's place looked almost exactly like my family home. It was a rectangular cement house with a living

My grandmother.

area and three bedrooms. They had a separate structure in the yard where Kgabo lived when he came home from work. Like us, they cooked outside and had no running water or electricity. I knew I would get a bedroom to myself since I was girl. The house wasn't dirty, but it was messy and disorganized. There were pots and cooking utensils here and there. Household items and food needed to be put in order. I could see why my elderly grandmother needed the kind of help only a strong girl could provide.

I remember I heard a door open. By then it was midmorning. Ernest and Salvation came out to the front room. Both were tall and thin; I was the same height or maybe a little taller than Ernest. I could see we were related.

"What's up?" Salvation said, and offered his hand.

Ernest did the same. "Hey. Welcome. Happy to have you here."

With that, my mother stood. I said goodbye to her. There were no tears from me, although I felt them. A part of me hoped that my mother would change her mind somehow. But I knew that would not happen. This would be my new home until it wasn't. My mother hugged me and cradled my face.

"You are welcome to come home whenever you want. Your home will always be there for you." She smiled and I could only nod.

Soon after my mother left, Salvation and Ernest asked if I wanted to meet their friends. I was glad they asked. If they thought I looked or acted different from other girls, they didn't say anything about it. I felt like they saw me and thought, Cool. Let's have fun.

It only took one day to understand what kind of boys my two cousins were, and I knew we'd get along just fine. They loved soccer and were just as adventurous as I was.

These two did not hunt, so I knew that part of my life was over, but there would be lots of other things to fill my time.

I went with my cousins to meet their friends. We were going to chill in the bush, listen to music, maybe take a swim. As we walked around the village, Salvation and Ernest pointed things out—where the shops were, their friends' houses. Fairlie looked almost exactly like Ga-Masehlong, only bigger. Where we had a thousand people, they had maybe twice or three times that. We walked past the houses and into the wild lands and arrived at a river where several boys our age were roughhousing in the water.

I was wearing the same shorts and vest I had arrived in. I looked around, took my top off, and jumped into the water, too. Then one of the boys asked me my name.

"What's up? I'm Thabiso," I replied.

"Thabiso?"

Thabiso is a boy's name. In Pedi, it means "happy one" or "one who brings joy." I was bringing joy with me that day. I could tell they thought I was a boy, so I figured I would go along with it. I mean, I was swimming without a shirt on and I had no boobs. I looked tough like they did. My voice sounded like theirs, too. They would have been ashamed to know they were naked in front of a girl. Neither of my cousins said anything when I said "Thabiso." In that moment, I knew Ernest and Salvation would let me be me and have my back as family. It was a good feeling.

Soon after that day, before classes started, my grandmother took me to the school to register me as a student. I'd be entering the seventh grade. I wore a T-shirt and a pair of my sister's jeans, so they were tighter than I liked. There were kids and parents everywhere. I saw a few of the boys I'd swum with out of the corner of my eye. My heart got going a little faster.

One of them spoke up. "Hey! Thabiso! What's up? You remember you swam with us?"

"No. I'm not Thabiso. I'm his twin sister. My name is Mokgadi. I don't know you." I looked at him as if I'd never seen him before in my life.

"You look exactly like Thabiso." This boy looked confused.

"Yeah. Because we're identical twins. Twins look exactly the same. Thabiso went back home." I shrugged my shoulders and turned back around. I don't know how I came up with that.

The boy walked back to the group and I was close enough to hear him say, "He says it's not him. This one's a girl. Named Mokgadi. Says she's Thabiso's twin sister. I don't know what is going on, man . . ."

All week I couldn't get this moment out of my mind. I knew I'd have to be myself for school, so I was hoping the boys would let go of "Thabiso." I liked those boys very much and could see them becoming real friends.

By the time the first day of school came, I already had a routine. I'd wake up around 5 a.m. and get the firewood going. As soon as the pot of water was boiling, I'd make a simple breakfast—tea, mealie meal (a porridge-like dish made from corn flour and water), some sweet bread. I'd washed and ironed clothes for the entire family on the weekend, so our school uniforms were ready. Salvation and Ernest would wear trousers and plain white button shirts, and I would be wearing the tunic—a dress under which girls would also wear plain white shirts.

My new school looked similar to my old one. Basic cement structures bordered a yard enclosed with wire fencing. Nothing different except the kids were older. I was the tallest girl in my class. I kept to myself. None of the girls introduced themselves, although I know they were looking and whispering about me. In class, I paid more attention to my surroundings than to the teacher, and I couldn't wait for lunch break so I could chill with my cousins and play soccer.

When recess came, I grabbed my stuff and walked out into the yard.

"Thabiso?"

I turned around. There he was. The same kid from the river.

"Hey, it's Mokgadi. Thabiso left for the city," I replied.

"I feel like you are Thabiso." His eyes searched my face and he rubbed his chin. "You were swimming with us in the bush. Now you are here wearing a dress." I could tell this boy's brain was turning in circles.

"Look, my man, I don't know you, OK?" I stared straight at him and set my jaw. "Never met you before in my life. I told you I'm Thabiso's twin sister. You were swimming with my brother. How can I swim naked with you if I am a girl?"

He didn't believe me, but he had no other choice.

Eventually he and the other boys accepted I was a girl named Mokgadi and I had a twin brother named Thabiso who had moved to the city. As time went by, the boys took me into their circle. By then I was playing soccer with them and it didn't matter that I was a girl. All that mattered was that I could play on their level.

Six months went by, and I knew the girl's uniform had to go. I didn't want to wear it anymore. I was tired of having to change out of the uniform every time I had a soccer game. Every minute I spent changing my clothes was time

2008. Seventeen years old. Spring lessons.
Nthema Secondary School.

2008. Senior year. Just taking pictures around the school.

I wasn't playing. And with the numerous responsibilities I had at my grandmother's house, my time for playing soccer was limited.

I remember the first day I came to school wearing a boy's

uniform. Some of the girls were laughing and whispering when they saw me. I didn't care. None of the teachers said a word about it.

When recess came, I walked over to my group of friends. They started whooping as soon as they saw me.

"Ha! We knew it!! Thabiso!"

"That's why you didn't take off your shorts that day."

I laughed. Yes, I thought, today is the day I retire this lie. "OK. Yes. I was Thabiso. You guys got a problem with it?"

My friends crowded around me laughing and pushing me around.

I was relieved it was over. Thabiso never existed. I could put my twin brother to rest. My friends always knew I was lying anyway.

CHAPTER SEVEN
WHERE I BELONG

I HAD BEEN A NATURAL CARETAKER IN MY CHILDHOOD
home. But at my grandmother's house, caretaking moved
to another level. I did laundry for everyone with my bare
hands. I smoothed out our school uniforms with a manual
iron I heated up on the wood fire. I did most of the cooking
and cleaning, and shopping. My cousins did stuff here and
there, when they felt like it, but for the most part they didn't
clean, cook, or care for my grandmother's animals. All they
had to do was go to school, have fun with their friends, and
play soccer.

Sometimes I'd refuse to make a meal or wash their
clothes. I'd run back to my birth village to visit my
family instead and leave them to see what it was like to
do for themselves. It wouldn't last long, though, because
I understood them, they were boys and it wasn't expected
of them. They didn't know any better. It also didn't matter

because I had been sent there to do these things for them. As a girl, it was my duty.

Still, I felt like a slave.

And I felt very alone, even though I knew my grandmother and my cousins loved me, and I had made great friends in Fairlie. I could not let go of the feeling of wanting to go, of wanting to be on an airplane to somewhere. I guess you could say my soul was restless. By my early to mid-teens, I was sure of what I wanted out of life. I wanted to have a wife, to have children, and provide for my family in Ga-Masehlong and for the new family I would one day build. I wanted dignity and respect and happiness. I still dreamt of sports stardom. I'd tell my cousins and friends that I was going places. I wasn't sure how, but I was going. My friends would laugh and tease me about the dreams I was holding in my heart. They weren't being mean. It came more from a place of just not understanding where I was.

Our native tongue was Pedi. We tried to learn English in school, but I would say I learned most of my English by watching American movies and cartoons. I knew that I needed English to have a shot at the world outside my village. It was the language you needed for entry into any university in South Africa. My family could not pay for me to have any schooling past high school, but I thought if I could speak and understand English well enough, maybe I could get a sports scholarship to a university. Even if I didn't become a professional soccer player, I would have an education, and I could eventually get a good job in a city.

I became more obsessed with sports. I missed my family, I missed my home and my friends, and playing sports provided a distraction from that absence I felt in my heart. Whatever the school had available, I played it. I loved baseball. I was a powerful pitcher, but also a good outfielder. I played basketball with the boys and netball with some of my girl classmates. I took advantage of whatever was offered. Not that the school had much. Nthema Secondary School was the same as my old one in that it didn't have any real sports grounds. The "basketball court" was a rocky field with shoots of grass and a rusted hoop where we also played soccer and baseball.

There were no coaches—our school didn't have money for that. Our teachers helped organize the teams and then supervised us when we played. I had a home-language teacher named Mr. Maseko, but we called him "Boss." He wasn't a coach, not officially, but he was a sports person. Boss would come watch us play and offer guidance and break up any arguments or fights between the kids.

Boss waved me over one day after a baseball game. "Mokgadi. You played very well today."

"Appreciate it, Boss."

"There's a new sport starting at the school next year. Athletics."

"Athletics?" I liked the sound of the word.

"Competitive running," Boss said. "You look fast out there when you're playing soccer and baseball."

I'd raced all the time, but never seriously. Just against my sisters and my boys every now and then. All of my siblings had run in school competitions, but it was basically like a physical education requirement. There was no official system that fed talented kids into higher levels.

When organized athletics started at my new school, I, of course, joined. I knew I was fast. I ran everything from sprints to 4 kilometers (about 2.5 miles), and I was faster than any of the girls in my school. I began competing against girls from other schools, and I was faster than most of them. Boss would encourage me to race the boys, too. I'd beat most of them because most weren't playing sports with the intensity that I was.

When I was fifteen years old, I'd just finished a practice when Boss came over. I was moving well that day, not fast, but strong, centered, and focused.

"Are you really serious about running, Mokgadi?"

"Man, running makes me feel free," I said. "I feel great when I'm running, Boss. I forget about everything in life, just forget about anything that bothers me. I love it. I really do."

Here's the thing I realized about myself—I am a human being who likes to be in my own space. I loved team sports, but it's hard to take a loss when you know you're doing your best and your teammate isn't. The worst is when your teammate *is* doing their best but it's just not good enough. With running, it's all on you. My mind was also never quiet when I was playing team sports. It was turned outward, if that makes sense. Running was different. My mind turned inward, toward itself. It quieted down. I felt completely at peace.

"Ah," Boss said, and looked at me in a way I hadn't seen before. I think that was the first time he saw me as a real runner. "OK, Mokgadi. I believe you are now ready to hear some things."

I was ready.

Boss said the greatest runners in the world came from Eastern Africa—Kenya, Ethiopia, Somalia. Then he told me that for pure speed the best sprinters in the world were Jamaicans and Americans. I sat with him, completely taken in by his words and the sound of his voice. It felt good to be spoken to by an elder man in this way, to be seen as someone worthy of his time.

I loved hearing Boss talk about the Kenyans especially, because they were the runners to be feared in long and middle distances. I remembered my parents told me that our tribe were descended from the Maasai, who are

Kenyan. Yes, I felt deep in my soul, this running thing was in my blood.

"Mokgadi," Boss said to me, "I believe that one day you will come across the great Kenyans. And what I am trying to say is, you don't know the power you have in you. That is your problem. Focus, child. Because you can be better than them. I see future in you." The corners of his mouth turned up, he gave me a slight bow with his head and walked away.

With these words, Boss changed my life. In that moment, it was exactly what I needed to hear. Soccer was like a great first love. Then you grow up and you discover what real love is. I knew I could not get to the level of success I dreamed of playing women's soccer. I couldn't provide for my family playing soccer. By now I also knew professional men's teams weren't going to let a girl on the team, no matter how well she played. But running was a different matter. There was fortune there for women. There was recognition. Competitive running had real opportunity for a girl like me.

As I became a regular in the youth running circuit, my body became more of a thing that was observed and commented on. I'd overhear coaches and other runners say, "That doesn't look like a girl," or "Why is this boy here with us?" I had no problem going right up to them and introducing myself. "Hello. I am Caster. I am a girl. Would you like to see? I can drop my shorts here for you."

That would be enough to shut their silly mouths right up.

I knew I was being carefully watched by the other girls. After races, as I'd head over to the facilities, many of the other runners would make it their business to walk in at the same time as me. They'd quickly grab their things and follow me. I'd strip and walk to the communal shower area and suddenly I would find myself surrounded by girls. They would stare at everything on my body. I was fine with it. I could tell some were disappointed they didn't see what they were sure I was hiding. Others seemed intrigued. They made awkward attempts at conversation during and after the showers.

One day I was sitting on a bench in the girls' facility after a regional cross-country race. I heard multiple people walk in and I looked up to see a runner surrounded by doping officials. (In certain leagues or competitions, runners may be tested for performance-enhancing drugs, to see if they are "doping.") I knew the drill. They were walking her to the toilets to watch her pee, and then they would test the pee for drugs. I was only fifteen or sixteen years old, but I'd already peed in a few cups myself. The doping officials would have you bring your running shorts down past your knees and get up close and personal with your privates because they need to see exactly where the pee is coming from to make sure you are not giving them someone else's.

The runner and I locked eyes. And that's when she said it. "What are you doing in here? What's a boy doing in here? This is the ladies' facility," she said in Pedi.

"So?" I said. "Yes, it's the ladies' toilet. You think I'm lost here? Why would they let a boy in the women's facility?"

Maybe it was the way I responded, because she suddenly looked embarrassed. I could tell she felt badly and it was an honest mistake.

"I see. My apologies. I meant no disrespect. What's your name?" She stood there kind of awkwardly. This girl was taller than most, but still several inches shorter than me. She was very thin, the kind of thin you see on the longer-distance runners. She was beautiful—glowing brown skin, high cheekbones, almond-shaped eyes, full lips—but I wasn't thinking of that in that moment.

"What's *your* name?" I said. "Introduce yourself first. You're the one who came in here disturbing *me*."

And at that, she laughed and so did I. She told me that her name was Violet Raseboya. She was a world-class cross-country runner from Limpopo. She was five years older than me, one of the experienced runners who'd already been overseas.

"OK then, Vioooolet." I drew her name out in a teasing manner. "I'll see you out there on the loops."

"What do you mean, little girl? You'll see me on which loops? What loops are you talking about? You think you can beat me?" Violet put her hand on her hip.

This Violet was a sassy girl. I liked that she wasn't intimidated by me.

"Yeah, I do. I'm lethal. Like a cobra." I gave her a half-smile. "I'll come over there on your side and dust you off one day."

The conversation with Violet was brief. I didn't think much of it or her afterward. She was the same as everyone else who'd assumed I was a boy, only she had said it to my face. I couldn't have imagined she would become one of the most important people in my life.

CHAPTER EIGHT
THEY SAW ME RUN

I HAD DONE SO WELL IN ONE OF THE DISTRICT RACES
that I had qualified to compete at a regional-level 800-meter
race. I knew that if I managed to win at the regional
level, then maybe I would be offered membership into an
official running club. By now I'd run enough and talked
to enough people that I had a basic idea of how things
worked. The running clubs fed athletes to ASA, Athletics
South Africa, our country's sports governing body, which
was in charge of creating South Africa's national team.
Only athletes who were members of ASA could qualify for
international competitions, and those races were regulated
by the all-mighty IAAF, the International Association of
Athletics Federation. ASA was affiliated with SASCOC,
the South African Sport Confederation and Olympic
Committee, responsible for choosing which athletes went
to the Olympics. The Olympics were controlled by the

International Olympic Committee, and their regulations basically followed the IAAF's.

The 800 meter is about the perfect balance between speed and endurance. You have to run at your almost-top speed, ignore the urge to give everything too soon, hold back just enough so you have some energy to explode with near the end. It's about something else, too. Luck. On this particular day, I didn't have it.

I was a back-to-front runner. I preferred to be in the back of the pack, watching and waiting. I knew how to stalk my prey. Then, near the end of the race, once I knew who the leaders were, I'd dig deep and do my best to outrun them.

In the middle of this race, I got spiked by another girl who was wearing track shoes. I was running barefoot.

Collisions happen, especially in the 800-meter race, because runners don't have to stay in their lanes after the first turn. Instead, we all come together, everyone fighting for a good position, trying to stay close to the inside, avoid getting boxed in, all while running nearly as fast as humanly possible. People get elbowed, pushed, spiked, kicked—sometimes purposefully. In the men's races, runners sometimes actually throw punches.

This girl had run over my foot, and her spikes had nearly ripped off my pinkie toe. I knew it was an honest mistake; she didn't mean to hurt me. But it was over. I came in fifth and limped off the field trailing blood with every footstep.

That loss started a fire in me. I should have won that race. I began training like a madwoman. I would miss my beloved soccer games, and I'd pass on just chilling with my boys in the bush.

Boss had a friend who worked in the athletics program at a neighboring school. The school was bigger, and they had a gravel track. When their students would practice, I would join in.

I had no coach of my own but I soaked up as much information as I could. I would go there and watch the other runners and imitate their training. I knew nothing except what I saw other runners doing and whatever information I could get from people I met in the running world. I had no fancy gym equipment, no nutritional supplements, no state-of-the-art running shoes, no orthopedic doctor and physical therapist at the ready to diagnose, treat, and massage injuries. Not even ice to put on sore muscles. Water was precious in our world because you have to walk several kilometers to get it. My feet were constantly blistered, the flesh torn up from being punctured by thorns and other sharp objects. I learned from older runners how and when to drain the blisters and keep going. The goal was to build tough skin.

When the holiday break was over, I returned to Nthema Secondary School and went straight to my principal,

Mr. Modiba. "I'd like to sign up for another year of athletics."

I could already tell by the look on his face that whatever he had to say wasn't good. Money is scarce in rural villages. Our school did what it could for its students, but the administrators were always juggling the little money they had for us.

"Mokgadi, we don't really have any runners here. You're the only one. We don't have any funds this year and we are ending the program. I am sorry."

I couldn't accept it. "Sir, I know I can do this. I just need a chance."

"I know. I'll see what I can do for you, but there are no resources. Perhaps, during your breaks, you can go practice at the other school as long as you keep up with your classes."

Mr. Modiba was as good as his word and would even give me rides when he could. I have always appreciated the way he took the time to help me.

I was running in as many races as I could get to and now training at a third school, Bakwena High School, about five kilometers away from mine. The teachers at this school could see I was talented and dedicated. They could also see I didn't have much of anything except my will to get there and run.

Just before a practice race at the school, I saw a man

walking toward me. I recognized him as one of the school's administrators.

"Hello, Ms. Semenya. I hear you are a very good runner. It looks like you'll be needing these." He was holding a pair of running spikes. The spikes weren't new, but they were new to me. I'd never owned a pair.

I felt so grateful. I thanked him and he walked away. I don't know how he knew my size, but they fit perfectly. To be allowed to use such a big resource as a pair of running shoes meant others believed I was going places. I did a few run-ups. It was a relief to know that I didn't have to think about rocks or thorns. My feet would be protected, even from other runners.

That day, I felt like I floated to the finish line. I won my 800-meter race, and then I sat and immediately took off the spikes. I carefully wiped them with what was left of my drinking water and my sweat rag. I made sure they were completely clean and then I found the school administrator.

"Thank you so much for letting me use them. I appreciate this very much," I said as I handed the shoes back to him.

The administrator looked at me and smiled. "Ms. Semenya, no need. Please." He held his hands up. "They are yours. They are a gift from us to you."

I was overcome with emotion. "Are you sure?"

The man just smiled and put his hand on my shoulder

and assured me they were mine to keep. I remember my spirit felt lifted. I was being seen.

From that day on, I used those spikes for every training run, for every race. They were my lucky spikes.

I eventually qualified to run in a national youth race. I would be representing the Limpopo province against the best youth from all over the country. I ended up with a silver medal in the 800 meters. It was the first time anyone from my province had won a medal at a national event.

After this, it seemed like everyone started talking about me, the girl who was running on another level. People would call my name in the stands or crowd around me after a race. If a girl like me, who did not even have a real coach, could win a silver medal at a national, I could do more. I made it my business to go up to running officials and sports coordinators in Limpopo before and after races to introduce myself and ask questions. I'd ask everything from how the running system worked, to how fast I needed to run to qualify for higher-level events, and where the next race would take place. In those days I didn't have the internet to rely on for information. I knew these were the people who could see me run and help me one day get a scholarship.

I understood that if I was going to make it in the running world, I had to give up everything else. Professional runners are professional runners. So I decided to quit all other sports, including my beloved soccer. My teammates were angry and disappointed, and they had no problem letting me know. They were about to lose a big piece of their game.

"Doesn't matter what you say. You can't understand," I'd say to them. "I can see light with my running."

Soon I qualified to represent South Africa at a racing event in the neighboring country of Botswana. I called my mom; she was surprised at the news. It wasn't that my family didn't know I was running, but they didn't think that it was a very serious thing. This would be my first trip out of the country, about a seven-hour bus drive. Aside from my father, who had visited several countries in Africa as part of our church's congregation, no one in my family had ever left South Africa.

I didn't do well in the event. I came in fourth, and to this day I don't know what happened except to say I couldn't find the zone. I didn't yet understand that racing wasn't just about being fast, it was also about strategizing and quieting the mind. I was used to running alone, my only company at times just cows and sheep and goats. I resolved to learn and never lose again.

Right after Botswana, I won a silver medal at the 2007 Confederation of School Sport Associations of Southern Africa championships, and I was approached by the Moletjie Athletics Club. The club was run by two men, Jeremiah Mokaba and Phineas Sako. I was sixteen years old. It was a big deal to be asked to join an organized professional running club like Moletjie—only the runners with true potential were asked. Most importantly, they were affiliated with Athletics South Africa. The only problem was that since I would no longer be running as a student, I wouldn't have access to free bus rides, so the traveling expenses and member dues would have to be covered by my grandmother.

My grandmother was proud of me. She saw my discipline and she loved the little medals and trophies I would bring home from my races. Even though she supported my passion, when I told her about needing to pay for transportation and dues, she didn't immediately agree. We had enough money to eat, but nothing more. My parents gave me what they could when I visited home, but they too had just enough to maintain the household. I'd taken to saving the few rand my mother would give me so that I could buy supplies, but it was not enough to pay my way to these high-level races.

Mokaba and Sako offered to come see my grandmother in person and explain things to her. I remember she told me she was surprised when these two men showed up. They sat in our living room and talked over tea.

"If she tries her best—and we have seen that she does that every time—there will be men with big bellies who can help her get a scholarship to a university," Sako told my grandmother. "She will be getting an education while running. And then she can begin to win good money to help the family."

The meeting worked. My grandmother understood that if these men were willing to visit her home and sit with her, then this was a real opportunity.

Now, for the first time, I would have people who were only focused on running and could help me develop and get me to the races that mattered. I ran everything, even the longer distances in the cross-country season. The first year, I qualified for the nationals in the 4-kilometer distance but I didn't do well—I was ranked thirty-four in the country. It did not matter; I didn't let it get me down. I knew what kind of runner I was—I was a pure middle-distance runner. The 800 and 1,500 meters, specifically.

CHAPTER NINE
ON THE WAY UP

MY WINNING BROUGHT MORE SCRUTINY AND questions about my body and gender. Other coaches would approach Sako and Mokaba and ask if I was really a girl. They would confirm that I was. Other runners would whisper about me. Some took issue with my running style; some resented that I seemed too powerful, too masculine. Even if I wasn't the fastest.

There was another major issue I would soon encounter. Race. I knew something about "the Struggle," as South Africans refer to the apartheid period. My father would sometimes talk about when they couldn't go into certain towns or cities, the humiliation of not being able to use public toilets or eat in certain restaurants. I was born in 1991, the year the IAAF allowed South African athletes to rejoin international competitions after the fall of apartheid.

I was born what is called free. Racism, the actual act of it, is something I hadn't directly experienced. There were no White people in my village or in Fairlie. I would see them from time to time, they'd come with equipment to dig for natural resources in the bush or set up electrical grids. But I'd never lived with a White person or had a real conversation with one.

When I arrived at the facilities for the cross-country 4-kilometer junior nationals, I went to look at the room list to see who I'd be sharing a room with. I saw the name of an Afrikaner girl (Afrikaners are the descendants of the White Europeans who colonized South Africa). I looked around for her. She was standing with her mother, also reading the room list. She looked at her mother and mouthed some words, and then she nodded toward me. I remember how her mother looked at me. I could tell, instantly, there was a problem. I watched as her mother went over to the registrant. They ended up paying for a separate room, and I had the room to myself for the event.

Was it because I was a Black girl? Was it that I looked like a boy? Either way, it did not hurt my feelings. They had the money to pay for a separate room so the White girl did not have to share one with me. What did it matter? I liked having my own space anyway.

I won the race. And with the national cross-country

4-kilometer title, I now qualified to attend the World Junior Championships, which would be held in Poland that July of 2008.

The only way I could get to Poland was on an airplane. This was it. The dream I had, the dream I held so close to my heart, was within my grasp.

The Moletjie Athletics Club was too far for me to train with them on a consistent basis. The majority of the time I was training alone, implementing whatever I learned on my own. We would get in contact only when we were approaching a specific competition they thought I should run in. Then I'd find a way to meet them and I'd train with the other runners in the club.

One of our training sessions to prepare for my trip to Poland was held at the University of Pretoria, about 400 kilometers away from my grandmother's village. It was a four-hour bus ride. Pretoria was a proper city, one that people like me dreamed of living in. My father worked in the city as a municipal gardener, but I'd never visited before. This would also be my first time seeing what a university looked like.

It was spectacular. The University of Pretoria's grounds were big and beautiful, and there was a place inside them called the HPC—the High Performance Centre—which housed athletes visiting from all over the world. My teammates and I were stretching and moving around on

2008. Running in an interprovincial cross-country race.

the grass surrounded by the track when I noticed an older Black man with a stopwatch in hand standing next to an orange plastic chair placed just inside the track's inner edge. He barely moved from his spot. He just stood there, clicking the stopwatch, blowing the whistle hanging around his neck, occasionally saying a word or two to his athletes. He'd look over at me every now and then.

I knew who he was. I'd seen him once the year before at a cross-country competition, and people talked about him. His name was Michael Seme. He was a Zulu man from Soweto, well known for helping runners achieve their maximum potential.

I was lying on the grass when I heard his voice.

"Hello there! Semenya, yes?" I turned my head and saw Seme wave and smile as he walked toward me. "I'm Michael Seme. I hear you are preparing for the World Junior Championships in Europe. I see you are a good runner. I can help make you great. Would you like to work with me?"

I looked at him. Part of me expected this, part of me couldn't believe it.

"I know who you are, sir. I need a coach. And I have no doubts about myself being great. If I join you, that means I would be a student at this university, yes? Then I would need a scholarship. I will run for you."

He asked me what school year I was in, and when I told him I was in my last year of high school, Seme said all I needed to do was graduate and he would do his best to get me into the school on a scholarship.

And that was the problem.

I had become a better student after I moved to my grandmother's village. I went to school every day. It was better for me to be in school than to be in the house doing chores. I was enjoying the lessons, but as I took running more seriously, I couldn't keep my grades up. Where I'd previously been an average student with average grades, now I was barely passing. More like failing.

I knew I had to dedicate myself to my studies, but first I had to go to the World Junior Championships in Poland and win. I arrived in Poland completely focused on winning. I was not going to repeat the mistake I'd made in Botswana. This was my first IAAF-sponsored World Junior Championships, and I was coming in at a disadvantage. My old injuries weren't properly treated. I couldn't afford any outside professional care. I was taping myself, bursting my own blisters, trying to figure out the best way to stretch pained muscles. I had never had the benefits of regular health care. Here, I got a taste of what professional athletes were offered in terms of meals and medical treatments in the Western world. Physiotherapy was available free of charge to all the participants, and I, of course, wanted some of this modern treatment. I told the therapist I was suffering with shin splints, and they went to work on me.

Unfortunately, I was in more pain after the therapy than before it. When I got to the track to run in the first heats, the pain was almost unbearable. I lined up with the rest of the girls, and I felt like a baby. These girls had already been running in the junior international circuits, and it showed. Halfway through the race, I tripped on the track's inner border lip and almost fell. I came in seventh and ran a 2:11:00. Not bad for a seventeen-year-old at her first international event, but nowhere near what I needed to move on to the final for a chance to win a medal.

I just needed the right conditions. I got another chance when I qualified for the 2008 Commonwealth Youth Games in India that October. I had three months to prepare, and I knew I would perform better because I was now training with other experienced athletes, and I had Sako and Phineas to show me the way.

When I got back to South Africa, I remember telling my cousins and friends, "See? You said I was running for nothing. I have already boarded a plane. I went all the way to Poland. I touched down in Europe. Now I am going on another plane soon. I am going to the Commonwealth Youth Games in India. This is how I will be signing my name in the future . . ." and I started signing my name in my notebook for them.

"Yeah, well, you didn't win, Caster," my friend Commy said.

But I could see how happy he was for me.

"That's OK. I'll win in India." I grabbed his notebook and signed my name on a blank page. "Keep this in a safe place, my man. That's going to be worth a lot of money one day."

My friends laughed but I knew they were proud of me.

I went to the Commonwealth Youth Games in India and I won the gold medal. My time was 2:04:23. Just as Boss had foretold, I beat the great Kenyans.

We had been given around eight hundred American dollars as pocket money when we went to India. I returned to South Africa with every single dollar. I never spent a cent of it. I had some plans for that cash, some things I wanted to buy. But instead, I helped my mom pay off some debts. It felt right to do that. After all, I did say I would be the one carrying the household one day.

Now, all I had left to do was pass my final exams and get into the University of Pretoria on a scholarship. I had neglected my studies so much that my teachers and the principal were worried I wasn't going to make it. But I wasn't worried at all. My view was that if I didn't graduate, I would just repeat my grade. I would take a break from running in official races, continue to train, focus on my studies, and come back to Michael with grades that would get me a scholarship. I would not be the first or the last student to have to repeat a grade.

Unlike many others, though, I had a good reason—I had won a gold medal at an international competition. The Commonwealth Youth Games, like the World Junior Championships in Poland, were IAAF-sanctioned events.

2008. Me with all my medals, the last day of school.

These were the big leagues. People knew my name now. I was officially in the record books. In my mind, I was well on my way to being a professional runner.

CHAPTER TEN

A HIGHER EDUCATION

I PASSED. MY GRADES WEREN'T GREAT, BUT I CALLED
Seme at the university and told him.

"Ah! Mokgadi. Congratulations. You will need to send me your school transcripts. I will apply for you here and let you know what happens."

A few weeks later, it was official. I was accepted to the University of Pretoria with a scholarship. If things went as planned, I'd be graduating with a one-year diploma in sports science. The scholarship covered school fees and accommodations. Seme would help me enroll in an additional program that paid for the things athletes needed, like food and health insurance. Student athletes in South Africa were also allowed to make money while studying, so I could run in any race I was invited to or qualified for and keep my prize money.

I would have a real coach, someone I would see every

day who cared about my progress, in a professional running system. I would learn about the kind of nutrition that was best for athletes, and my injuries would be treated by experts. I would have access to a state-of-the-art gym. And I didn't have to worry about that thing that had burned me for so long—watching my cousins Salvation and Ernest just live their lives while I slaved over the household.

Before I left for Pretoria, I went back to my birth village of Ga-Masehlong, back to my parents' house. I knew this would be the last time I'd see my family for a long time. It was early 2009. Both of my parents and my siblings and nieces were there to see me off. They knew I was on the path I had seen for myself.

I was eighteen years old and full of the hopefulness, bravery, and certainty about the future only a young person can have. There were no tears from me. I don't cry. I do a lot of things to show how I'm feeling. Crying is not one of them.

My mother hugged me fiercely. She looked at me like she always did, with the deep knowing only a mother has.

"Take care of yourself. Don't worry about anything or anyone. Your home will always be here. You will always be loved here. Don't stay away for too long."

I wondered if maybe my mom and dad felt that my

being a different kind of girl would make me a target outside Limpopo. I showed myself to be a fearless kid in the villages, but my parents knew a little more about the world than I did. When you are older, you have more knowledge—about the past, about the way people had been and the way people can be. They remembered the times our people, Black people, weren't free.

I walked out of my first home and sat with our animals for a while. It had been almost six years since I'd really taken care of them. Some had died, some had been born while I was living in Fairlie. I took in the sight of everything—our home that always felt like it was falling apart and yet still stood strong. Our small patch of land where we grew just enough fruits and vegetables to sustain us. I closed my eyes and listened to the music that was always playing from somewhere, and I saw myself once again as a toddler running and falling and flying. I saw myself being chased by my sisters.

Before leaving, I spent some time with my childhood cousins and friends—the first boys I'd loved, the ones who taught me to hunt and swim and who accepted me as one of them.

"Have time for a game, Mokgadi?" one of my cousins said.

"Why not? I could beat you again."

A small crowd of villagers gathered around us. They shouted "Mokgadi! Mokgadi! Mokgadi!" as they had done when I was a kid. Maybe a few placed bets. They knew I was a sure thing. There was still no one who could handle this girl.

I traveled the next morning to see my maternal grandmother. This is the grandmother I am named after. It is our custom that when we are to embark on a long journey, we must seek the blessing of our living elders as well as our ancestors. My grandmother and I prayed together. I could feel the joy, anticipation, anxiety, and hopes of my family. I was carrying the dreams of our people.

I arrived at the University of Pretoria at the beginning of February 2009. I had turned eighteen in January.

At this point in my life, the fastest I'd ever run an 800-meter distance was 2:04. In order to be considered a top prospect and qualify or be invited to senior-level events, I would have to run much faster than that.

Michael Seme and I got started on my technique right away, and he was an excellent coach. He first wanted to understand what I had been doing, mostly on my own, to bring me to this point. And I told him. I was doing the things I'd seen athletes at bigger schools with actual tracks do. I told him I would run by myself when I wasn't taking care of my family home.

I remember Seme nodded and then just added to the

foundation I'd laid for myself. He found my running form to be too loose, he felt I swung my arms too much and held my head too far back. He would eventually help me get to the form that made me a winner—arms locked in close to my body, chest high, head centered.

Seme had us start a training session every morning at 5 a.m., and then we'd go to classes and have a second training session at 4 p.m. I was getting frustrated about my constantly losing to the other girls at the school, so Coach had me go up and down this steep hill that surrounded the track. Up and down, up and down I went until my legs burned past the point of pain and I couldn't breathe at all. As I got stronger, going up and down the hill became easier until it felt effortless. It would eventually come to be called Caster's Hill.

I spent my days training and getting acclimated to living in a bustling metropolis, a world that was very far from the small village surrounded by wilderness I'd come from. I remember one of the first things the university did was to have the new students take a tour of the city. Our guide showed us the places where just a few years before Blacks had not been welcome. I looked at the public parks and bathrooms, the stores, the museums, and marveled that I had made it all the way there.

I also began to see more of the runner I'd met a few years prior: Violet, the senior runner who'd mistaken me for a boy in the women's facility. Violet had begun coming to Pretoria on the weekends to train with Seme and became part of our group. We'd spend time together and began a real friendship. Violet had been nursing an injury, but at only twenty-three years old, she'd already represented South Africa at the World Athletics Cross Country Championships in 2005, 2006, and 2007. She was living and working in Soweto and was in a relationship with a guy who lived there. Because she was from Limpopo, being able to spend time with her made me feel less homesick.

During an 800-meter event at a Yellow Pages event (a South African racing series), I won in 2 minutes flat. I knew that one day I would run faster than my personal best (PB) of 2:04, but I didn't think I would hit the 2-minute mark so quickly after I began working with Seme. With just one officially certified 2-minute run on the books, my life began to change.

The day after my win, Michael said he needed to talk to me about something important. And that something important was money.

"Caster. I am your coach. My job is to condition your body and help make you great. You see how you ran the two minutes. You will get even faster. So now you need someone to take care of your business. To bring you more opportunities. Things I cannot do for you."

"OK," I said. I knew what he meant. I knew the best athletes had sponsors, companies that paid them, and this could lead to many more opportunities, like being the face of sports drink, shoe, and clothing brands.

A middle-distance runner I greatly admired said I needed a manager who was interested in building me as a human being and told me that he would send his agent my way. This agent was a man they called Madala. To us, *madala* is an affectional term that means elder. His actual name was Jukka Harkonen, and he was a well-established Finnish sports manager.

A few days later, we had a training camp at the university's High Performance Centre. Jukka was there, and we officially met in person. Jukka made me feel safe. He said he'd heard great things about me and that he would like to see how he could help me. He did not take out a contract and try to pressure me into hiring him as my representative. He said that he first wanted me to think about what I wanted in my life, what I wanted to achieve as an athlete, where I saw myself in the future, and that we would speak again soon. I knew I wanted to sign with him. Here was a man who never once mentioned money. To me, that was a real businessman.

A month later, I met with him again. He was holding two packets of paper, one in each hand.

"Caster, I hope you have thought about the things we discussed. I have two offers for you from two companies. Adidas is in my left hand and Nike is in my right hand. Take a look and let me know what you think."

Before Jukka could hand over the papers, I said, "I don't care what's inside those contracts. I'm going with Nike."

"Are you sure? Look through them and see first."

"Nike," I said. "That's the one for me."

Today, I am still a Nike athlete. It was one of the best decisions I ever made.

With the 2-minute run in Germiston, I had qualified to run in the South African Athletics Championships held in March at the Coetzenburg Stadium in Stellenbosch, a town in the southwest part of my country. This annual competition was organized by ASA, and it would be my first senior-level event. At eighteen, I was still considered a junior runner, but I would finally get to see what it was like to run against more mature athletes and even meet the runners who would eventually make it onto the senior-level international stages where the real fame and fortune were.

At Stellenbosch, I won the 800 meters with a time of 2:02. Seme had traveled with me, and he was so happy because I was getting faster. With this victory in a senior-level event, I was officially a professional runner.

Best of all, I had also been given a spot on the national team that would soon take me to the world championships in Berlin. I would be representing my country at the highest level in my sport.

I was satisfied. I knew I was on my way. I knew I could hang with the big guys.

CHAPTER ELEVEN

THE TROUBLES BEGIN

WHILE MY FAMILY KNEW I WAS ABOUT TO COMPETE IN the African Junior Championships in Mauritius, I never told them I'd also been given a spot on South Africa's national team and that I was going to Berlin. To me, Berlin was an animal to be dealt with at a later time. The African Juniors were for athletes aged nineteen and under; Berlin was the major leagues. I've always been the kind of person who likes to deal with what's right in front of them. I try not to worry about the future, about things I cannot control. This way of being is what I believe prepared me for what was to come.

I won gold in both races at the African Junior Champs. I ran the 1,500-meter race in 4:08:01—a personal best and a championship record. And in my favored distance, the 800 meters, I won in 1:56:72. I'd never run so fast in my life. It was another personal best, a championship record, a national record, and a world-leading time that year in both the junior and senior levels.

I called Seme from my room, and he couldn't believe it. I told him I ran a 1:56 and he yelled, "A WHAT? A 2:06?" I repeated a 1:56, but his mind couldn't process it. "Ah! OK. Did you say a 1:58 or 1:59?" And I said, "No! A ONE. FIVE. SIX. Coach." Seme was quiet for a second and then started hooting.

What I remember clearly of this moment in my life was a feeling of inevitability. That everything I had worked hard for was about to come true. People in the South African athletic world were really talking about me now. I was the new kid on the block. I had thrown down a 1:56 at the age of eighteen. That was only two seconds behind the time of Pamela Jelimo, a Kenyan who was the entire game at that point in middle-distance athletics.

The Berlin world championships would take place two weeks after the African Champs. This was it. I was going to compete on the international stage. This would be the biggest race of my career. The gold medal came with a $60,000 cash prize. I don't know if I thought I was going to win so much as I believed I had earned my right to be there. But if I won that gold medal, or got anywhere near it, it would be the beginning of so much more in my career. I would get invited to even more lucrative races. I could be offered more sponsorships. And I knew my Nike contract came with incentives and performance bonuses. I could see my life as a famous athlete right in front of me.

The world championships are the premier IAAF event—more than two hundred countries send their best athletes. It is held every two years, and the lucky host country usually sells hundreds of thousands of in-person stadium tickets for the multiday event. Millions upon millions of people around the world watch the televised event.

I wasn't nervous about performing or being seen by millions of people. The truth was I didn't even know who my competitors would be—except the Kenyans, Pamela Jelimo and her countrywoman Janeth Jepkosgei. Those were the only two I thought about. Seme and I had created a plan for how I was going to tackle the heats and the final. I was there to run fast, stay out of the pack, try to grab the gold medal and bring it back to South Africa.

I even started to think about what kind of signature move I would make if I won. My favorite wrestlers like Lex Luther, Hulk Hogan, and the Rock had a move they made when they won. Running wasn't wrestling, but it was still a show, and I wanted to give the audience something special.

I finally came up with something. I'd spent most of my childhood in the bush. I was a hunter and a herder. I grew up respecting nature, and one of the animals that commanded the most respect and fear was the cobra, one of the deadliest, most venomous snakes in the world.

Yes, I thought, I'm lethal . . . like a cobra—that is my running style. Once I decided to strike, to make a move on the track, no athlete could keep up with my pace. So I would bring my arms up and flex my biceps. I'd hold that pose for a second or two, then flip my wrists out and open my fists so that each of my hands looked like the striking head of a cobra. And since I'd killed off and buried my competitors, I would then cross my arms over my chest and use my open palms to "brush the dirt off" my shoulders. I also loved eagles. Eagles were strong and defiant. You can't take something away from an eagle easily. When I held my arms out, they also looked like wings. Eagle wings.

OK, I thought, looking at myself in the mirror, I've got something going here.

I was ready to show it off to my best friend.

Violet's job had transferred her to Pretoria from Soweto, so she was now living near the university and still training with Seme. It was great because we hung out all the time. We'd chill a little bit, talk, cook together, watch some TV, listen to music, and crack jokes. Violet had broken up with the guy she was seeing before she moved.

I knew I had feelings for her, but I wasn't sure if she had feelings for me. Didn't matter. Our friendship meant more to me than anything else.

She came over one night after I was done with classes and training. Berlin was a few days away.

"I have something to show you," I said.

Violet had that look on her face when she knew I was getting ready to say or do something crazy—which was often.

"OK, so I was thinking I needed a signature move for when I win the championship."

Violet started laughing. "OK, Caster. Let's see it." Then she stared at me wide-eyed like a kid about to see a magic trick. I had her undivided attention.

I took a few steps in place like I had just crossed the finish line. I made the whooshing sound of the crowd applauding me. I went through my cobra-eagle hybrid moves and ended it with the shoulder dust. I may have even added a kiss and a peace sign for extra dramatic effect.

Violet just sat there and continued to stare at me. And then, like my sisters had many years ago, she shook her head and said, "Caster. You really are crazy." But I could tell she liked it.

Then Violet got up and went over to her bag.

"I brought you something," she said, and handed me a folded piece of cloth. I thought it would be a T-shirt or a blanket for the plane. It was the South African flag.

"For when you cross the finish line first," she said.

I took the flag and held it up behind my head and ran around my small room. I was already in Berlin; I was already on the winner's podium.

The day before I was to leave on August 7, I got an early morning phone call. Seme told me ASA had reached out. They were sending someone to meet with me about "some tests." He didn't say what tests, and I assumed it was another doping test. I was used to those.

An hour or so later, I heard a knock on my door. Michael was there with an older White woman. They walked into my room, and I closed the door and sat on my bed. Both Michael and the woman stood.

"Hello, Ms. Semenya. My name is Dr. Laraine Lane. I am a psychologist with Athletics South Africa."

I wasn't expecting a psychologist. Michael's face didn't look one way or the other, so I couldn't get anything from him. Dr. Lane seemed nervous. She kept rubbing her hands together as if she were washing them. I kept thinking things didn't feel right.

"You should be very proud of yourself, Ms. Semenya. Everything you've accomplished up to now. Your family is proud. Your country is proud. But, you know, people talk. That's what they do. They will always talk. We don't know what the results of the test will be, but you should be proud of yourself."

"OK. But what is it that they're talking about? I will be taking the test and the result will be that I don't do drugs, so we can just go ahead and move on from this. I'm packing. I'm leaving for Berlin tomorrow."

Dr. Lane took a deep breath.

"Well, the thing is that you may not run in Berlin, Caster. It happens sometimes this way. Over things we can't control."

"Well, since I'm not doing drugs, and I can control taking drugs, I don't see why," I said to her.

At this point in my life, I was just a young village girl. But I was also stubborn. I didn't know what she was talking about, and I really didn't care. All I wanted was for her to leave so I could keep packing.

"Caster, they are going to run tests on you at the Medforum hospital in Pretoria. Today. You can't get on the plane to Berlin without taking the tests."

"That's fine. I'll go to the hospital. Because I am getting on that plane." I was thinking that they'd take my blood, take my urine, see I am a clean athlete, and this would be over and done with.

Not long after she left, I went to the hospital alone. A nurse met me in the waiting area and escorted me to a patient room. There were two chairs and an examining table with what I now know are stirrups, the foot supports a woman uses during gynecological appointments. I had never seen those before. She directed me to the chair. Soon

THE RACE TO BE MYSELF

an older Black man entered and introduced himself as Dr. Oscar Shimange, a gynecologist.

"Yes . . . Hello. What's this?" I pointed to the table. "I'm here for a doping test, Doctor."

Dr. Shimange sat in the chair across from me. He looked at me and brought his thumb and forefinger up to the bridge of his nose.

"No, Ms. Semenya. Did these people not tell you what you are here for? You are not here for a doping test."

Looking back, I can't say this is the moment I knew what was happening or about to happen. I knew something didn't feel right when the psychologist came to see me, but I never imagined it would be this.

Dr. Shimange, unlike Dr. Lane, didn't talk around the truth. He came straight out and leveled with me.

"Look, I'm going to be honest with you. It is my duty as a doctor to do no harm. I have been asked to perform a gender test on you. It is your right to refuse to take this test."

I knew what the word *gender* meant and so I wasn't bothered. I felt something more like annoyance.

"Ah. This thing again. OK then. What's the problem? Do the gender test, Doctor. Let's not waste time. I have a plane to catch. A gold medal to win."

"Ms. Semenya, this isn't as easy as you think. I'm required to do a full examination."

"OK. Then do it," I said. "What do you want from me? You need to see my things?" I leaned back in the chair and crossed my arms.

Dr. Shimange took off his glasses. "Ms. Semenya . . . are you a boy?"

I laughed. I'd been accused of this before. "I have nothing to hide, Doc. I'm a girl. I have only girl parts."

Then I undressed, put on a hospital gown, lay on the examining table, and spread my legs for the first time in my life to another human being.

Dr. Shimange looked at my privates, but he never touched or asked me any questions during the exam. I couldn't tell from the expression on his face what he was thinking. Then he brought out a sonogram wand and placed it on my lower belly. (A sonogram is an imaging technique used to look at internal organs, tissues, or—during a pregnancy—a fetus.) He drew blood and then the exam was over. Once he was finished, I got dressed and we spoke as two humans, not as doctor and patient. I could tell that he was a good man.

"Caster . . . I am going to tell you the truth here. You are not built like most other women. I know you already know that. But these people are looking for a specific issue . . . a hormone in your blood called testosterone. Both men and women have this hormone, but you may have a higher level of it than the sports people allow for your gender. I am sorry . . . I think the results will show this is the situation with you, Caster. As a fellow African, I have to tell you . . . I think the chances of you running in the world championships are very low."

I just sat there and listened. He went on to mention "chromosomes" and "X's" and "Y's" and how sometimes certain functions are blocked in the body when there is a hormonal imbalance. The words and science were beyond me at the time. I'd never heard these terms before, and I didn't hold them in my mind. Still, I understood he was saying that even if I was born a girl, I was different because of this hormone.

Once he was finished, I spoke.

"It is God's will, Doc. It's a part of life, this thing you say I may have. If I have it, God gave it to me. I've been able to live my life and be successful with it. I don't see why this would be a problem now. I've been running in the system this whole time. All I know is I am a girl. I don't have a penis. You saw that with your own eyes. That's all I know. You can finish your tests. If they say I can't run, then I can't run. But they haven't stopped me yet. Thank you for your time."

I called Violet and asked her to meet me in my room. I needed my friend. When she came, I told her everything.

"These people lied to me, Violet. They should have just told me they didn't want me to run. Just straight up, like that. Just say it. Wasting my time, my whole day. Invading my privacy. Looking at me down there. Talking to me as if I am something less than human."

I was walking in circles around my small room. "They are here trying to say I'm not a girl. Maybe I just won't go. If this is what is going to happen, I'd rather just stop now than force myself into an environment where I am not welcome." Then I sucked my teeth. "That's one part of me. The other part of me says, *Forget them.* I'm going to the championships, I run this thing. I trained hard."

And with that I was done. I felt like my fury had died down a little bit. I sat on the bed and just held my head in my hands.

Violet, my soft-spoken, softhearted friend, was listening as only she did—intently and without interrupting me. Once she sensed a pause in my venting, she suddenly burst into tears and began sobbing.

"What is this? Why are you crying? I am not crying. I am angry. There's no need for you to cry. Please, Violet, don't cry." I put my arms around her.

Five years older than me, Violet understood—more than I did, I think—what the implications were. After all, she was the first competitor who ever told me to my face that she thought I was a boy. Her running career was on hold because of her injury, and she needed to work to provide for herself and her family. I knew it meant the world to her to see me succeed.

Violet gathered herself. "Caster . . . please, listen to me. You are young. Too young to deal with such things. I am sorry this is happening to you. But remember you are an incredible person. I've never met anyone like you. Go to Berlin and enjoy yourself. You worked hard to get here, and you deserve the chance. Win or lose, you earned the chance to be there. Focus on yourself. Everything will be fine."

Violet spent the night with me. We talked late into the night. The next morning, we said our goodbyes.

Whatever doubts I'd had the day before were gone. I was on my way to Berlin.

CHAPTER TWELVE

BERLIN

ON THE FLIGHT TO BERLIN, I TRIED TO RELAX AND NOT think about the gender test the day before. I had not discussed it with anyone but Violet. It was something I just wanted to put away. Almost something I didn't want to believe had happened.

The doctor had told me there was a chance I wouldn't be able to run based on the results of the test. I didn't know when those results would come out. Still, I was determined to make the most of the opportunity that had been given to me. I couldn't or didn't want to believe that I would be disqualified because of the body I'd been born into.

The heat I'd be in was probably going to be 2.1 or 2.2, meaning between 2 minutes 1 second and 2 minutes 2 seconds. If I hit that, I would move on to the semifinal. I'd need to dip under 2 in the semi to make it to the medals. If

I made it to the final . . . I would win. In my young mind, that was all. Simple.

The 800-meter heats were held on August 16. I just needed to keep up with the Kenyans. One was Pamela Jelimo, the only woman who scared me. Jelimo had that 1:54 on her legs; the fastest I'd run was 1:56, and I'd only done it once, and only two weeks ago. The other Kenyan was Janeth Jepkosgei, the reigning 2007 world champion. That woman had run 1:56 several times over.

My Berlin experience could well have ended the day of the heats. Two hundred meters from the finish line, Jepkosgei was leading and I was right behind her, on her right shoulder. I wanted to pass her, so I made a move to the outside. Jepkosgei moved at the same time. I don't know if she realized what I was trying to do and didn't want to let me go by. I accidentally clipped her heel, and she fell. It was an accident borne of my inexperience; I was staring straight ahead, unaware of my surroundings, and I wanted to come in first. I ended up winning the heat in 2:02:51. Jepkosgei recovered but came in last.

Unfortunately, I also had a problem with my right leg again. I twisted my ankle when I tried to jump over Jepkosgei's falling body on the way to the finish line. It hurt terribly, and I limped my way back to the locker room.

After the heats, I went back to my hotel room. My

mind was on my ankle when I heard a knock on my door. It was the vice president of Athletics South Africa, Attlee Maponyane. Such a high-level representative would usually not be visiting an athlete's room, but in my case we were close because Maponyane was from Limpopo. He'd been the president of Limpopo Athletics when I was running in the districts, and he'd taken a liking to the kid who was never afraid to follow him around after events and bother him with all kinds of questions.

"Caster, how are you feeling?"

"My ankle hurts. But I'm feeling good. I ran well." I was sitting on the floor, icing my ankle.

"Caster, now . . . look, this is not easy for me to say, but these people don't want you to run anymore."

"Who doesn't want me to run anymore? I'm fine. I can still run with this." I expected he was going to say something like, there was no need to blow my leg off at my first-ever world championships.

"People are talking. The IAAF is concerned you may have some kind of issue in your body. They want you to withdraw. Maybe they won't let you run. I think it's best you take yourself out. You can just be done with it now."

Maponyane looked at me the way a parent looks at a sick child—with affection and concern. It was clear to me by the way he was talking that he knew about the gender test in Pretoria.

I shook my head and continued icing my ankle.

"You made it all the way here and you won the heat, Caster. You proved yourself. Now your ankle is hurt. You are young. You will have more opportunities."

But what more opportunities could he be talking about to a girl like me? A girl who had made it all the way from a village in South Africa to the world championships in Germany and had just won her first heat? What better opportunity than this one, right here, right now? A gold medal and a cash prize for my family?

I had to run. That was the only answer.

"NO. I'm going to run. If the IAAF wants me out, they will have to come drag me off the track. I came here to win."

"Caster, these things are complicated. We are hearing the results of the test will not be good. I don't know what it means for you . . . we don't know what will happen if you continue. What we can do is bandage your ankle. Tell these people you are too injured to run."

I've said before that I don't cry. To me, tears are useless. I know how to swallow them. This was one of those moments when I couldn't hold them back, and I didn't want to.

What I felt in that moment was that if I did not run, my life was over. Not over in the way a teenager feels like their life is over because they can't go to a party or they want something their parents can't afford. I felt like my life would be over in the sense that whoever I was and whoever I was meant to be would cease to exist.

Attlee knew I wasn't an emotional person. I saw in his face that seeing me this way moved him.

"Caster . . . things are in such a state we believe this is for the best. Your ankle is hurt anyway. You can go now and we sort this out at home," he pleaded.

"Who would it be best for? Why should I withdraw? Because of what? Where are the results? What have I done wrong?" I asked him.

Maponyane seemed like someone who was trying to handle something but did not know how to. He explained there were no results from the test but that even if I ran in the semi, these people could disqualify me.

"I see my name is still there," I said, pointing to the television. "They could have disqualified me after the heat and they didn't. I worked hard to get here, sir. I don't do drugs. I don't know what this thing is about and I don't care. My business is to run. Let *them* disqualify me. But not you. Not my own people. Your job is to support me."

And here, I stood and leaned against the desk in my room.

After a few seconds of silence, Maponyane brought his hands behind his head.

"Caster, what happened in South Africa, the test . . . the IAAF wanted it done there and they will do it again here. Even if you go through the semis, Caster, you will have to do their test to run in the final. Do you understand? Do you know what's coming? Are you prepared to deal with that?"

"I am prepared for anything, Attlee. Whatever's coming, I'm ready for it. What I know right now is I'm going to run. I'm going to reach for that gold medal. I will go home after that. The rest will follow."

Maponyane came over, put his hands on my shoulders, nodded, and left my room.

Go home or run. The choice was a simple one.

On August 17, 2009, I woke up, put on my gear, got on the team bus, and headed to the Olympic Stadium. My ankle still hurt but it felt better and I could run. None of ASA's officials said a word about me not running. I stayed quiet. I stayed in my own mind. I didn't eat. I still don't eat before races. I didn't strategize with a coach. I knew the plan for the semi—stay in the front, avoid a collision, dip below 2:00.

I remember walking out to the track, warming up. I could feel the heat of the other runners' eyes. They were watching me closely. Whispering amongst themselves. Occasionally I'd look back at them to let them know I was aware they were watching me. Nothing more. It didn't matter to me. Whatever they were thinking was their business.

If the gender issue came up in my mind, it appeared

as something completely ridiculous. The whole thing made no sense. Whatever these people said was in my blood did not take away the fact that I was a girl. One thing at a time—right now, the track was there, the finish line in front of me. Just get through this, I thought, one step closer to the gold.

I won the semi—1:58:66.

Jelimo, the 1:54 runner I was most wary of, had been nursing an injury and jumped out halfway through the race. She would not be in the final. Jepkosgei came in second. I'd beaten the great Kenyan to the line for the second time.

Now the young girl from Limpopo was getting all the attention. I remember being surrounded by reporters and cameras. Now they were interested in my life story—where I came from, how many siblings I had, what my parents did for a living. I answered as best as I could. My English was rusty, and there were things I obviously couldn't understand.

I was nervous, not used to being asked so many questions, not used to having cameras so close to my face. All I wanted was to take a shower and eat with my teammates. I wanted to go back to my room and chill, listen to music. I couldn't wait to call Violet and tell her I had won. That we were one step closer to the gold.

And I almost made it. I'd just walked past the barrier

that blocked the media from walking into the locker room when a reporter called out to me. I stopped.

He was a middle-aged White man.

"You have improved tremendously in your times. With that comes rumors . . . there is one that you were born a man. What do you have to say about stuff like that?"

I took a breath. Even knowing what I knew, I was thrown by the question.

"I have no idea about that thing . . . I haven't heard about that thing. Who said it? I don't care about it," and I walked away. I was angry. What kind of person asks something like this of another? Here I was, a kid, and some adult man was questioning my womanhood while holding a microphone.

I told no one about what had happened. If any of the team heard about it, no one mentioned it. I remember getting back to my room. I talked to Violet, but only about good things, positive things—I told her how I was going to win now that I had a spot in the final. I was just starting to loosen up in my room when an IAAF doping official came to take blood from me. Maybe they were taking multiple samples from all the athletes, but to me it felt personal. I knew the plan was to disqualify me, so maybe they were purposefully trying to annoy me, to get me to withdraw, and avoid some scandal at such a high-profile event. It didn't matter. Until someone from the IAAF came to me and said, "You can't run," I was going to ignore them.

I went to bed dreaming of gold medals.

August 18 was supposed to be a rest day. I remember my phone rang early that morning. It was our team coach, Wilfred Daniels. He told me that the IAAF needed me to take some tests at a nearby hospital and that he would come with me.

I met Daniels outside our hotel. We normally traveled to and from the stadium and hotel on regular buses, but this time the IAAF did not want me to take a bus to the hospital. They had sent a black car with tinted windows. I see . . . I thought, They need to keep this thing quiet.

When we arrived at the hospital, a woman met us in the waiting area. I was to follow her, and she motioned that Wilfred should stay. I remember we took an elevator ride that seemed to go on forever, and when we walked into the patient room, there was an almost identical examining table and the stirrups. There were several medical personnel in there—I don't remember how many or what each of their titles were. None of them spoke English, or maybe they pretended not to.

"What am I here for?" I asked. I knew what I was there for.

A translator turned to me. "Ah. Yes. They need to value you, Ms. Semenya."

"Is this a gender test?" I asked. I knew it was.

I don't remember the reply. It didn't matter. What did any of it matter at that point? I had to go through with whatever this was because I was going to run in the final.

"OK, you want to see my vagina? Do what you need to do. Let's get on with it then. You are wasting my time."

I don't know if they knew my words were rude, but they understood my tone. No-nonsense. What was happening here wasn't respectful, anyway.

I took off my clothes and put on a hospital gown. The room was chilly and smelled like it had just been disinfected. I lay on the table and placed my legs in the stirrups. Unlike the doctor in Pretoria, who never touched me, one of these doctors came right over and began to pat around my vagina with a gloved hand.

"You won't find what you are looking for. You won't find it because it isn't there."

I decided to taunt them with my words. I wanted to irritate these people in the way they were irritating me.

Then one of the doctors brought out what I now understand to be an internal sonogram wand and handed it to the one who was doing the examination. The doctor made a sort of motion with it that was meant to communicate to me that he was going to put it inside my body.

"*No. No.* You're not putting that inside of me."

I waved my hand and shook my head no in case my words weren't clear.

There was more talking, and the translator turned to me. "Very sorry. Must for procedure. Check inside."

What I knew in that moment was that if I didn't let them look inside my body, I wasn't going to be allowed to run in the final. This wasn't about me having a vagina. They'd just seen it with their own eyes and touched it. And this also wasn't about something in my blood, because they had plenty of my blood already. So why did they need to look inside my vagina? It was one thing to spread my legs and let them look and touch me, but this, *this* was a whole other level.

I have only discussed what happened in that room once, in the version of this book I wrote for grown-ups. You are young. I have young daughters, and I try to protect them. Maybe someday soon you will want to read about this test, or maybe your parents will let you now. I want to hold nothing back. I am direct. But you are innocent, as I was then. So all I will write is that, on that day, they did the test.

But I made them do it *my* way, and they did not get what they wanted.

Later the doctor got a different wand, with a flattened top. This one I recognized from the South African doctor's office. He placed it on my lower belly. It tickled. When he was finished, they took more blood and urine.

More blood. I remember wondering if I had any blood left in me to run the final. They took my blood after the heats, more blood after the semis. Now, again, blood. For now, though, it was over. I put on my clothes. The translator silently accompanied me to meet Wilfred in the waiting area. She had me sign some paperwork. I don't remember reading it. It didn't matter. I didn't care. We took the car back to the hotel.

I told Wilfred soon after we got in the car. I told him because I trusted him. Even though discussing something like that with a man who wasn't even part of my blood family was inappropriate. In that moment, I just had to tell someone.

"I thought this whole thing was about doping, but these people really think I'm a boy. Same thing here that happened back home. They had to look at my privates again."

I didn't tell him exactly what they had done, but he looked pained and stunned. I remember he made a sound, the kind of sound we make when we feel shame but also helplessness. We didn't speak any more about it.

The other athletes were eating, laughing, calling their families and friends. Rest days are for unwinding our minds and bodies. I went to my room and slept. I didn't call Violet that day.

August 19, 2009—the day of the finals. The test made me all the more determined to win. All I cared about was winning now. I had an opportunity to do something great. This was my chance, and no one was going to take it from me.

About an hour before the final, I got to the warm-up area. I could feel something had shifted in the air. Because someone at the IAAF had "accidentally" told a journalist about my gender test, reports about it had been all over the television. I had seen many of them. And so had everyone on the track.

Normally, I don't care who looks at me. I was used to being looked at; I was used to being whispered about. The other runners had ignored me when I first arrived and then seemed more interested after the heats and semis. They were experienced runners, champions, world-class athletes. To them, I had come out of a jungle a month before to qualify for the championships. No one had given me the time of day, or a chance, until they saw me run the heat and the semi. But today, there was something else in their eyes. It was fear. The only thing they saw in me was *fearlessness*.

The call room is the final place where all athletes gather prior to taking the field and lining up. This is where IAAF officials come up and check your outfit, make sure you're wearing legal spikes, make sure you are not bringing anything you shouldn't onto the field. The athletes are in very close quarters here, usually loosening up, stretching. You can hear everything. What they said specifically doesn't matter. I knew they were talking about me, laughing at me. It probably made them feel better to make fun of me when the reality was they looked like they wanted to poop their pants.

My plan for the final remained the same. Give it all I had. Forget everyone else. I felt relaxed, totally chill. I didn't need to stretch. I was ready. I crossed my arms and sat back in my chair with half-closed eyes. Someone came, checked our outfits, bibs, shoes. Then they moved us to the tunnel leading to the stadium. Still, more talking, more whispering about me. My upbringing, my very nature, had conditioned me to take in these kinds of situations and pass through them.

The truth is I came to Berlin hoping I would be in the top five. Maybe even top three. I would get some experience, go back home, work on getting faster. But now, I knew I was going to win.

Finally, we were let out onto the track. We were introduced to the spectators. I knew the rumors about me being a boy were going around; I knew what some people were thinking when they called my name. Here is where the feeling of shame and embarrassment would have caused most people to crumble, to cry, to walk off the track even. But not me. I just took whatever this was and let it brush off me. I lifted both hands and waved to the crowd.

Like all other athletes, I shook off the nerves at the line; I release them as soon as I take my stance, settle into my lunge, bent at the waist, left leg forward, waiting to go. Just the year prior to this one, I hadn't yet learned to quiet my mind. I would sometimes talk to myself at the line, trying to bring myself under control. But I felt myself in a different space after being and learning with Seme. By the time the gun went off, my mind was totally blank. I was not thinking of anything at all. I didn't hear any sounds at first.

I was in lane four, three from the inside. The first 200 meters felt too slow, so I jumped out. Jepkosgei came with me, and we were side by side for a few steps. She tried to take over, but it seemed like she changed her mind and hung back. I think she remembered I was eighteen and had a 1:56 on my legs, and she needed to conserve her energy. At 400 meters, I made my move.

Now I was flying.

When I heard the final bell, signaling our last lap, I made sure I was out in front of the pack. Then I took over. I could see the finish line. I remember I turned my head slightly to make sure there was no one near me, then I started to pull away. The sounds of breathing and the pounding of the

Me getting ready for the 12th IAAF World Championships, which started in Berlin on August 16, 2009.

other athletes' feet faded away. I could hear the roar of the crowd around me. No one could follow me in those last 200 meters. I did what I had been training to do.

The little girl from a tiny village in Africa had won the gold medal in 1:55:45. Jepkosgei came through to win silver almost two seconds behind me.

Right after I crossed the finish line, I remembered to do my winning move. I hit the Cobra. I knew Violet was watching back home. I knew my family would soon know. I raised the South African flag Violet had given me and did a victory lap around the stadium. Whatever came after this didn't matter. If I was disqualified, it wouldn't change the reality of what had just happened. No one could take this feeling, this moment away from me. I would always be there, my win had been captured on video, seen by millions of people. I'll go home happy now, I thought.

This is where my story as an athlete truly began. And even though the best day of my young life would turn into an international scandal, I want everyone to know that I would do it all over again.

CHAPTER THIRTEEN

NOT WOMAN ENOUGH

AFTER MY VICTORY LAP IN THE STADIUM, I WENT BACK to the hotel with the team. There was a party with great music and plenty of food. Everything was beautiful. I had accomplished my mission—I had come up against the world's best that year and I had beaten them. Soon I'd come home and celebrate with my family, is what I was thinking.

At some point, though, things started to look a little different. I did not attend the winners' press conference with the silver and bronze medalists right after the race. I'd had no idea there even was a press conference to attend. Pierre Weiss, the IAAF general secretary, had sat in my place and proceeded to discuss my gender and what might or might not have been happening with my body.

"There is a question of whether this person is, in fact,

a lady," Weiss had said. He followed that up by saying the tests they'd done so far showed I was "clearly a woman, but maybe not one hundred percent." There were questions from the media about whether I would be allowed to receive the gold medal at the ceremony the following day, since the results from the gender test could take weeks. Because I hadn't been immediately disqualified after the race, I didn't know there was ever any question about my receiving the medal. I was busy enjoying the fact that I had won.

I spoke with Violet and never once mentioned anything about the test. I told her about the excitement of the competition, how ready I'd been. Looking back, it's hard to believe, but aside from what I considered the stupid gender test and the conversation about withdrawing and the possibility of being disqualified, nothing seemed out of place to me. Those had been the only discomforts.

The next day, August 20, I went back to the Olympic Stadium to receive my medal. I felt proud. Accomplished. For me, it was the culmination of my hard work. Like any other race I'd won. I remember they called my name and put the gold medal around my neck. The crowd roared their appreciation of my performance. It was an amazing feeling to stand on the highest podium and see them raise South Africa's flag and hear our national anthem.

We were in Berlin for a few more days. I cheered on my teammates and mostly stayed in my room. I sometimes watched myself being discussed on television. I would sit in my bed just staring at the screen, hearing the way the television people from all over the world were talking about me. To me they weren't real. I just didn't understand what the fuss was all about.

We left Berlin on August 24. What I did not know was that from the moment the IAAF confirmed that I'd been gender tested, media from all over the world had already reached out to anyone they even suspected of having ever been within two inches of my person. Newspapers were already filled with quotes from people in my life, including my parents, who brought out my birth certificate and a copy of my passport to prove I had been female since birth. People at the Berlin airport recognized me. Some yelled congratulations, while others pointed at me and whispered to each other.

By now my teammates knew what was going on. The whole world knew. They did their best to protect me on the way back home. I was the baby in the group. I remember how they tried to keep me from seeing the newspapers in the hotel and in the airport. That was an impossible task. The world championships were watched by millions of people in almost every country, and a half million tickets had been sold just for the stadium. So many amazing performances that year and Caster Semenya's genitals seemed to be the main story.

In the immediate aftermath, I was not hurt in the sense that I was going to sit around crying or get myself down about it, but I was offended. I felt disrespected as a person. I came from a place where people minded their own yards, where gossip was seen as the devil's work. It was just incomprehensible to me how people could discuss such intimate matters in public in this way. It felt like I came from a different world, one that operated with different rules. And the thing that made me angriest was that it felt like I was being called a cheater. I hadn't done anything wrong.

By the time we arrived at the airport in Johannesburg on August 25, IAAF had leaked the initial results of my blood tests to the international press. When I landed, the newspapers had even more fuel for the fire—they reported that tests showed I had three times the testosterone level of a typical woman. The speculation was that I was either a boy or a hermaphrodite, meaning someone with both male and female parts or physical characteristics.

That intense scrutiny is the opposite of what I received at OR Tambo International Airport. When I walked past customs, it didn't feel like an airport at all. The place had been transformed into a concert. Thousands of people were jammed inside the arrivals area. It seemed like every media outlet in the country was there, along with every major politician. I was in shock. Music was blaring from everywhere. People were singing, shouting, dancing, waving the South African flag, and holding up printed and handwritten signs that said: OUR GOLDEN GIRL; CASTER, YOU ARE A BEAUTY; CASTER, YOU GO GIRL; OUR FIRST LADY OF SPORT. Others were holding up newspapers with my birth certificate plastered on the cover and a headline that read

YES! SHE'S A GIRL!!

Airport security and policemen surrounded me and my teammates. They tried to get us through the crowd, but were no match for the people swarming around us. They pushed their phones in my face, trying to touch me, hug me, kiss me. I remember people grabbing and yanking on my tracksuit. I was being swept this way and that by the mass of people.

I knew this was a celebration, but nothing seemed right to me. I'd won gold, but the celebration seemed to be about something other than my actual win.

The national team finally made it onto the double-decker bus. It was one of those open-top buses, and it circled the airport so we could wave to the crowd. I kept being reminded by others to smile and wave. And I would occasionally do so and hold up my medal for everyone to see. But then I would suddenly go blank and the smile would just slip off my face. Part of me wanted to celebrate with my people, to just be joyful. The other part kept asking,

What is it that I've done wrong? The only thing I've done is be an athlete and win. Now all these people are saying there is something wrong with me, they are saying I'm a cheater. That I don't deserve the medal.

The bus ended up at the airport's parking lot. A stage had been set up there. So many people were there, including my entire family. That was a beautiful surprise. They were standing shoulder to shoulder with famous politicians I'd only ever seen on television. There was Winnie Madikizela-Mandela, our beloved Nelson Mandela's former wife. She was a member of Parliament and a much-loved figure in her own right. There was Julius Malema, the head of the African National Congress Youth League. I always loved

Crowds of people gathered at OR Tambo International Airport to welcome me and the South African national team.

THE RACE TO BE MYSELF

Fans welcome me back to South Africa.

to hear him speak on freedom and revolution on television. I remember thinking that all of these big people, whom I'd never met in my life, seemed to love me as if I had been born in their household.

OK, I thought, this means I matter the most. Let me carry on, enjoy this moment. Even if the truth is that, for me, it was not enjoyable. I was there with everyone, but at the same time it felt like I wasn't there.

We got off the bus and onto the stage. There's a singer who prompts me to do my signature winning move. The Cobra. So I do it.

Be happy, I remind myself. Look at what you've done for your people.

Smile. Dance. Wave. The outside world thinks I'm

a cheater, they are saying something is wrong with me, but here, my people are celebrating me. So ... it's OK, I reminded myself, I don't care what other people think. Stay here, be present, with your people.

Then there was a press conference where politicians each took turns speaking about how my human dignity had been violated. Everyone seemed to support me and my right to run. They saw in me an innocent Black child caught in a terrible situation. For them and all of us, it became about more than gender—it became about race. It became about

2009. At OR Tambo International Airport in Johannesburg with Winnie Madikizela-Mandela.

White people coming and telling us Africans what we were and what we were not based on our looks—the same categorizations and violations of human rights that were happening during apartheid. I became a symbol of how Black people have been violated and exploited throughout history. Would this be happening to a White European teenage girl?

I just sat at the table. Thinking of nothing. This thing was beyond me. Thinking of just getting some sleep.

We were then taken to the presidential guesthouse in Pretoria. The national team was to meet the president of South Africa, Jacob Zuma. The president made a short speech about how proud he was of the South African athletes and the five medals we had brought back. But my teammates' accomplishments were once again overshadowed by my plight. The media only wanted to hear about me. President Zuma addressed what he called my public humiliation and said that I and my family had the country's full support. I remember staring at my hands while he spoke, wishing I were somewhere else, even though to be there was such a great honor.

I was asked to speak, and it was the first time I was able to address the media directly. I remember saying it was good to win the gold medal and bring it home. I talked about taking the lead at the 400-meter mark in the race and how I celebrated in my mind at the 200-meter mark because I knew none of the other runners could catch up to me. This is what I imagined speaking to the media in Berlin would have been like had I been given a chance to attend the winner's press conference.

A journalist asked President Zuma if the IAAF was going to take the medal away from me.

"They are not going to remove the gold medal. She won it. So the question does not arise. There's no worse that's going to come," President Zuma confidently said.

He was wrong about that. There was, indeed, plenty worse to come.

But before it came, there was one more person I got

Celebration in Ga-Masehlong upon my return from Berlin.

Celebrating with friends from Ga-Masehlong.

to meet because of my win. An icon of freedom and perseverance—Nelson Mandela. I grew up loving him and what he represented. I never dreamt I would one day meet him face to face. By then, he was ninety-one years old. He told me I was special, to not allow this discrimination to stop me from accomplishing my dreams. He said I was a great athlete and that I'd made him and the country proud.

"You are strong, Caster. I believe in you. You must believe in yourself."

In the moments of darkness that were to come, I remembered his words. If someone like him could survive and overcome twenty-seven years in prison and become a symbol of love and freedom to our people—why couldn't I endure this? What I was going through seemed like a small thing compared to what he had survived. Compared to all those who had died during South Africa's struggle for independence and democracy.

A few days later, on August 30, I traveled back home to Limpopo to celebrate with the people I'd grown up with. It was the same story. I was there, but I was not there. The village was full of people—many familiar faces and many faces I'd never seen before. There were more visits from politicians; even our village king paid a visit to our family. My parents greeted and fed visitors day and night at their home. I did everything I was supposed to do. I posed for pictures and showed off my medal. I caught up with my childhood friends whom I'd missed so much after I moved to my grandmother's village. And I ate and ate and ate. I'd missed my mother's cooking.

My family was so proud of me. My sisters were in the front yard of our home showing reporters the medals I'd won before becoming world champion. My mother and father were freely talking to journalists because there was nothing to hide—they gave birth to and raised a girl. Their view of the whole thing was that the White people had gone crazy and that we were not going to listen to anything they were saying. That was it.

Yet I can only imagine what my mother's heart was

My mom at the front door of our kitchen.

feeling. This woman who had given birth to me and changed my nappies and taught me so much about kindness, and humility, and strength.

I had promised my family I would make something of myself, that I would bring honor and provide for the Semenya clan. In the immediate aftermath of the win, I became South Africa's golden girl, but I didn't imagine that my tremendous victory would also come with whatever this was.

CHAPTER FOURTEEN
THE NOTHINGNESS

AFTER THE CELEBRATIONS IN MY VILLAGE WERE OVER, I returned to the University of Pretoria. All I wanted was to go back to my room and see Violet. I missed my family, but Pretoria had become my home, my own space. I was done with celebrations.

Toby Sutcliffe, the acting director of sport and the CEO of the university's High Performance Centre, met me as soon as I arrived at school. I'd become very close with him. I still call him "dad" to this day.

"Caster, we've decided you'll have to move out of the regular residential sports houses and into the HPC. It's the only way to keep the media away from you. They are everywhere and there's not much we can do to stop them," he said.

And he was right. Journalists and cameras were everywhere. Large groups of them at the gate of the school, others hanging off the fence that enclosed the school's track. Some even tried posing as students and faculty. Every one of them hoping to get a look at me and hopefully get me to talk. I wouldn't be able to rest if I stayed outside the school grounds. I'd be safer at the High Performance Centre, which was located inside the grounds with its own restaurant, offices, and workout facility. For anyone to get in there, they'd have to go through at least three different reception and security stations.

Toby introduced me to a guy named David who worked in guest relations at the university. David was assigned to bring me whatever I needed and to keep everyone away from me. He was to stay by my side from the moment I woke up to the moment I went to sleep.

While I was getting settled into my room at the HPC, the media storm continued to rage. It didn't matter to me. What mattered was that I was able to run in Berlin and win the gold medal. And now, all I wanted to do was go back and run. I wanted to show the world I did not become a champion by mistake.

Occasionally I'd speak to Violet on the phone. She didn't know what to say to me except to stay strong and that this would pass. I wasn't able to see her, and it was for the best. Toby said no one but my family should be around me.

On September 8, the IAAF announced they'd have the results of the gender test in two weeks. They confirmed there was no doping issue and I would get to keep my medal, although they still hadn't released my prize money. I was relieved about the medal, of course, but I still had to wait for the results. And I was curious. I had always wanted to know what was going on with my body. I never thought anything was wrong, I loved the way I looked, but I wondered why I was a different sort of girl.

Now someone else had found out the answers for me.

An Australian newspaper got ahold of the IAAF's gender test results and leaked them. There it was. What I did not know about my body.

I discovered, along with the rest of the world, that I did not have a uterus or fallopian tubes (the tube-shaped organs through which eggs travel from the ovaries to the uterus). The newspaper reported I had undescended testicles (meaning testicles inside my body) that were the source of my higher-than-normal levels of testosterone. They went on to call me a "hermaphrodite." In my culture, this term does not apply to people like me, but the world media forced that label on me and that is what I am called to this day. Sometime later, the term would change, and some people would refer to me as "intersex" and as having a DSD—a disorder or a difference of sexual development.

I had only been home a few days. I'd hoped that things would begin to quiet down and normalize themselves, and then suddenly, with the release of that news article, it was as if some kind of bomb had exploded . . . and the fallout just kept getting bigger and bigger.

I was on the cover of every newspaper, discussed on every single television station and radio show in South Africa. And the explosion wasn't just in my country: my face and story were plastered across television screens and newspapers all over the world. It was as if the entirety of humanity had discovered that some kind of alien that looked like them but wasn't them had been living amongst them. That's what this felt like.

I remember thinking, Now what? What does this all mean? What are the implications of it? Am I going to run again? Am I going to get my money? My mind raced through these questions and more—

OK . . . so this explains why I haven't gotten a period. Now I know it will never come.

This is why my hips aren't rounded.

This is why I can gain muscle quickly when I work out.

All right, if these people are saying I don't have a womb, then this means I will never be able to carry a child. I want a family. I can still raise a child because I have many nieces and nephews.

Well, thank *God* . . . I don't have to endure the pain of childbirth.

God made me. If he allowed me to live when I was born, he made me this way for a reason.

CASTER SEMENYA

Reports said I was immediately placed on suicide watch because I was ashamed and afraid of myself and afraid of what would happen to me now that my "secret" was out. That wasn't true. I wasn't suicidal at all. I wasn't afraid of myself. I was angry because there was no need for the world to know my business.

Looking at it another way, whoever leaked the results did me a big favor. I now knew what was going on with my body. I had top-level medical information, free of charge. I thought of all the people in the world who were like me and who would never have access to this kind of knowledge. At least I knew. And now everybody else knew, too. And if everybody knew, that meant I never had to talk about it if I didn't want to. And I didn't want to. I was done talking. All I wanted now was to switch off my mind. Just stop time.

The South African government tried to do what they could for me. Politicians came together and approved a grant so I could build a house next to my parents' in our village. The government also announced they would file a human rights violation petition with the United Nations. Winnie Madikizela-Mandela and Julius Malema were saying this all felt like a racist European system trying to deny a Black girl child her win and suppress her talent.

Life at school was totally different now. As the days passed, the lush grounds and state-of-the-art facilities at the HPC seemed more like a prison. Before, being here was my freedom, my way out of my old world and into a whole new one. My life had been about nurturing my talent as a runner, and now I was being called names and laughed at just because of how I was born.

My days felt empty. I was supposed to still study, to still train, to continue life as before while waiting, endlessly waiting, for what the IAAF would decide to do with me. Toby, David, and the rest of the staff tried to keep me occupied, keep me motivated. But I didn't want to do anything but be alone and sleep and think.

I slept most of the day and stayed up all night staring at the walls. And I'd watch the Berlin championship. Over and over and over again, I'd watch myself win. I studied every angle, every turn. Obsessively. I don't know why. Maybe to remind myself that I did win, that the gold medal was mine. Some would call this a depression. I didn't understand it as such at that time.

My sister Olga would come to see me. She would just sit next to me in my room and not say a word. So would Violet. They would bring me food and just stay quiet and let me be.

Toby sent a psychologist to see me. Her name was Monya. She was a sweet woman, but no match for what was going on inside me. We had a few conversations, but there was no getting through to me.

I think only the people who have faced what I

experienced can understand what I am talking about. How do you explain what it feels like to have been recategorized as a human being? That one day you were a normal person living your life, and the next day you were seen as abnormal? I was a young girl who'd been physically and emotionally violated by a system—a system that I had no choice but to exist within.

Imagine you are told one day that because of some medical this or that, you are actually not a woman. Think about it. In the eyes of the entire world, you are now something other than what you know yourself to be. And the entire world will not stop talking about you. Ever.

Black people all over the world know this feeling well; we understand it intuitively—the feeling of being different, of being othered just by virtue of existing. Black women, we understand it on a whole other level, of course. This is why my South African people were so horrified, why my newly democratic government threatened a third world war if my medal was taken away. We had freed ourselves from a system that kept Black people uneducated, kept people apart and broke up families. Uniformed White men had gone around and assigned people a racial identity based on what they believed you to be; they had the power to recategorize you.

Anger, I knew. Anger, I understood. What I was feeling then wasn't just anger. It was like a hole that threatened to suck me in. I kept thinking, This thing can never be undone. The girl I had been before I got on that plane to Berlin—happy, joking, innocent, eager, hopeful—she'd been disappeared on the way back. And in these early days of my exile, there was nothing to put in that empty space.

The only times I could leave the school was when I was invited to high-profile dinners and lunches with politicians. I didn't want to attend these things, but I knew I had to. I understood that, in many ways, my career was also in their hands.

My coach would do what he could to get me out of the room and back on the track. He would stand outside my bedroom window and call out to me almost every morning and evening.

I couldn't do it. If he called my cell phone, I wouldn't answer or I would tell him I had a headache.

"Look, what's the point of me training if I won't be competing? I don't see the use. Give me time on my own just to think about what I want to do," I'd say.

Everything I'd worked for seemed so far way. A world champion and now nothing. All I could do was wait. And pray.

The wait—and the nothingness—had lasted a few weeks when Michael Seme came to me and said Toby had received a call from two big-time lawyers based in Johannesburg—Greg Nott and Benedict Phiri. They wanted to speak with me to see if they could help me. I trusted Toby, and if he let them through to me, I would give them a chance. I didn't have anything to lose.

I remember the day of the meeting. Greg Nott was a White man who seemed to be somewhere in his late thirties and was the CEO of the South African arm of the law firm Dewey & LeBoeuf. Greg was an avid runner and had been deeply involved in South Africa's democratic rebuilding after the fall of apartheid. Benedict was a young Black lawyer who'd been raised in circumstances similar to mine.

Greg told me he'd watched the championships live with his son. He told me he had been overcome with emotion at how I'd been humiliated in front of the entire world. Greg said their legal position was that the IAAF had violated my human rights. Their idea was to sue the IAAF; they were sure they could get me a good settlement and would represent me pro bono, which means I would not have to pay them.

I thought about this. If they sued the IAAF and I won money, then what? They would go back to their offices in the big city with their share, and I would return to my village in Limpopo with the rest of the money, and that would be the end of it. I had a family to help support. I was only eighteen years old. How long before that settlement money ran out? And anyway, I knew what I wanted. I wanted to win. I wanted to go to the Olympics. I knew I could get there. In my mind, I was already there. I was a champion.

So I took a deep breath and finally looked up at them.

"I want to be a three-time Olympic champion. I want to be a three-time world champion. This isn't about getting money. I want to run. I want to win. That's it. That's the only thing I want. To get back on the track. If you can do that for me, then yes, I will be your client."

I could see that both Greg and Benedict were taken aback by my words. Greg said they would discuss the situation with their associates and get back to me.

They soon came back. They were serious about helping me. Now the real work would begin, and even though I couldn't see the future, I had a glimmer of hope that with these men in my corner, surely I would be able to run again.

CHAPTER FIFTEEN

HOPE

A FEW WEEKS LATER, IN NOVEMBER, THE IAAF FINALLY shared the results of my test with my lawyers. Greg came to see me to discuss what had already been leaked to the entire world. I don't remember the particulars of the conversation. It all came down to what the German doctors had found—my body produced too much testosterone and I couldn't compete as a woman by the IAAF's standard. Greg also explained the scientists had determined I had typically male XY versus the typically female XX chromosomes. (XY and XX are some of the many chromosomes found in human DNA. In most cases, XX means a fetus's sex is female, while XY means male. With a girl like me, that wasn't the case.)

Greg asked me if I wanted to take the papers.

"No. Burn them. I know my body is different. I am

Caster. I will forever be me. All I want to know is how I can get back on the track."

I refused to even touch the folder on the table. To this day, I've never seen the medical reports. Greg did as I asked and destroyed them.

"So what now?" I sat back and looked at him.

The IAAF offered only one solution.

"Caster, they want you to have an operation called a gonadectomy to remove the organs that are producing the testosterone. This will bring your hormone levels down. Then you can run in IAAF-sanctioned races again. I am not advising you to do this, I am only telling you what they are saying."

"That is their offer? To cut me open? You can tell them I said to go cut out pieces of their mothers. What kind of nonsense is this?" I got up from the chair. I was furious. Disgusted.

By then Greg knew me, and he knew I didn't hold my tongue. He knew I meant what I said. In my culture, operations are dangerous things. Who in their right mind would cut their body open unless something was wrong with them? Unless they were injured or dying, and the operation was the only thing that could save them? It was madness. If I had internal testicles or gonads or whatever they were saying I had, they were mine. I was going to keep them for as long as I wanted. This is how I was born. I loved my body. I was healthy. My body was strong and it had made me a champion. Why must I go now and mutilate it because some German doctors said there was something wrong with me?

I now know there are female athletes who have come before me and after me who have agreed to this solution, and they are changed forever. And when they become sick, when they can no longer compete and aren't winning medals for anyone, they are abandoned. There is no "retirement plan" for these girls. They are simply discarded and forgotten about.

For example, Annet Negesa was a promising Ugandan middle-distance runner. She was a three-time national champion and had qualified for the 2012 Olympics at only twenty years old. Despite having already competed in multiple IAAF races, she received a call while training for the Olympics, telling her they'd found elevated testosterone levels in her blood. Annet claims she was told by an IAAF doctor, a Dr. Stéphane Bermon, that to get back on the track was a very easy procedure. She alleges no one told her of any possible complications, nor that this "easy procedure" would involve surgery and how that would affect her life. She returned to Uganda for the treatment and maintains she believed she was going in for an injection but woke up with deep cuts in her abdomen, having undergone a gonadectomy. She never ran competitively again.

There are many more runners like Annet, almost always women of color, who have undergone these procedures to keep competing. I have run with these girls. I have seen them before and after. Some are trying to get back to where they once were, but you can see the light in their eyes has dimmed. I think about these girls sometimes—girls with little formal education, desperately trying to understand what is "wrong" with them and how in the world they are no longer considered women enough to compete. They are scared, alone, with no one to fight for them. Many don't even speak English, and there are no proper translators—they are already intimidated by a system they cannot understand. They don't have any resources to fight for themselves. Many others do not live in communities or societies that accept these differences, and they are afraid of what will happen if such news about their bodies were to become public. Many of these women, from impoverished backgrounds, see running as their only hope of making a life for themselves and their families. If they are told that the operation will at least give them a chance to continue in the running circuit, they will do it.

Only later do they realize the operation was a mistake.

I will forever be grateful for Greg and Benedict's incredible efforts on my behalf during this time, even if I didn't truly understand the scope of the process. These people saw an injustice and stepped in to help a young village girl, free of charge. They fought like warriors. Greg assembled a team, an international army really. There were American lawyers with sports law expertise working alongside the South African team, and others who specialized in human rights law. I remember they organized a medical team to discuss the findings with the IAAF's doctors. I even traveled to Istanbul with Greg, Benedict, and my coach Michael for more negotiations with the IAAF.

Once it became clear the IAAF was definitely not interested in going to court and having to publicly explain how exactly they've historically dealt with women like me, the discussions moved to a different battlefield—our medical team versus the IAAF's medical team. The point was to prove that despite my condition, I was still a girl. That something else, besides an irreversible surgery, could be done to keep me running.

A private gynecologist Toby knew in Pretoria had conducted a medical evaluation of me and joined our team in negotiations with the IAAF. She, along with others from our medical team, argued that if the issue was my testosterone levels, they could try to use estrogen (a reproductive hormone that produces typically female characteristics) to bring them down and regulate them. She warned everyone that there was no research on elite athletes with my specific physical condition taking estrogen just in order to run competitively.

My doctor cautioned about the immediate side effects and the possible long-term ones. Weight gain, blood clots, leg cramps, weakening of bones, vaginal bleeding, a general feeling of illness, breast swelling, headaches, sweating. She advised me that I shouldn't take the medication for longer than four years. I remember her saying, "Four years. That's it. You get one Olympics. Anything beyond that and you could do irreparable harm to your system."

I didn't care about the side effects at that time. I was only eighteen. I was young and strong, and I thought I could get through anything. As long as I wasn't taking anything out of my body, it didn't matter to me if I added hormones.

Greg and Benedict were concerned about my well-being, but they said they would offer this solution to the IAAF with the relevant medical data to prove it was worth a shot. They asked several times if I was sure I wanted to do this. I was sure. No lawsuit, I just wanted to get back on the track. I didn't consult with anyone about my decision to take the drugs. I just told Greg and Benedict to tell the IAAF that I would take the medication and see if it worked. If it didn't work, then my running days were over.

The IAAF said I would have to take it for at least six months, until my levels were "normalized." They would send their people to randomly monitor me, and then, once they were satisfied my levels were low enough, I could run again. They would also keep my medical records sealed, and no one would know what my exact condition was or how it was being managed. That was the deal.

And I took it. I told no one, not even my parents. Only Violet.

I would do two sets of blood tests a month—one for the IAAF, one for my doctor. And the IAAF reserved the right to show up whenever they wanted, as many times as they wanted, for random blood draws. That would be my life for the next several years.

I started feeling sick as soon as the drug was introduced into my system. At first it just felt like I'd eaten too much of something. My muscles felt heavy, and I was always tired. I couldn't recover from workouts in the same way I had before. My head would hurt. My brain felt cloudy. I was nauseous for no reason. The foods that I normally enjoyed, I no longer enjoyed in the same way. And I would suddenly get hot and start sweating. The thirst was unbearable. I'd have a gallon of water next to me in bed, and I would go through it desperately and then have to use the bathroom a million times. The hunger became its own challenge. Food is important for athletes; we eat more than most, but this was insane. I felt like I was starving all the time, yet I wanted to vomit. It was enough to drive anyone mad.

I could work around it, I constantly told myself. I had

no choice. I wanted to run, and this was the only way. The physical effects were there, but the medication was also messing with my mind. I was a sleep-deprived teenage girl. No longer my usual self. The self who cracked jokes on the track, did her best to focus in class, tried to see the positive in things, and believed in herself was being destroyed.

I eventually had to tell my parents and siblings what I was doing. I couldn't keep it from them any longer because they could see I wasn't the same Caster. I wasn't happy anymore. It broke their hearts.

I remember how much Violet cried when she saw me suffering because of the medication. She also begged me to stop. But I didn't care if the drugs were destroying me. If I stopped poisoning myself, then my life had no meaning. I'd have to start again from nothing.

After my birthday on January 7, 2010, I decided to settle something deep within myself. This was my life, and I had to live it as best as I could. I still had a chance to do something great. I would remind myself that even with the medication, this was still my body, I was still me. I knew what I was capable of. All I had to do was what I'd been doing my whole life in one way or another—fight.

I began training on a more consistent basis. Even with the drugs, my body was responding well in practice, and I was making competitive times.

The IAAF hadn't officially banned me, but it was

2010. With my parents on my twenty-first birthday.

understood I couldn't run internationally. We hoped I could run on South African soil, with the blessing of ASA, while the pills were taking effect. We tried to enter a Yellow Pages series race in Stellenbosch on March 10, 2010. The Yellow Pages series were run by the South African federation, not the IAAF. The IAAF had a new acting president, and despite making a bunch of noises to the media about how "athletes were the most important" and he was there to "take care of the athletes," he called Seme to tell him I should not run until things were settled with the IAAF. It didn't make sense. When my coach tried to register me for the race, the organizer immediately changed the entry to "invitation only." Since I hadn't been officially "invited," I couldn't run.

This here is a moment where I can fully say I was deeply hurt. I was turned away at the door by my own people. I was not a quitter. It just wasn't in my nature. When I started something, I needed to see it to its completion.

We put out a rare statement to the media that Greg and Benedict helped me craft:

I have been subjected to unwarranted and invasive scrutiny of the most intimate and private details of my being. Some of the occurrences leading up to and immediately following the Berlin World Championships have infringed on not only my rights as an athlete but also my fundamental and human rights . . .

Soon after this, the IAAF finally released my prize money. I felt an immense sense of relief and joy. Luckily, I had someone to share that joy with: Violet. Everyone still thought she was my "best friend," but we had become romantic. It hadn't been easy for her. Violet was scared, as she had never had feelings for a woman until she met me.

At the time Violet and I got together, I can't say

same-sex relationships were common or generally accepted in my country. I had never felt unsafe in my village even though I'd made it clear to everyone I was only interested in women. But the world was much bigger than just my village, and I would come to understand this kind of prejudice soon enough. For now, though, I loved Violet and I knew she loved me back. Here at least was a thing that was going right in my life. Something I was sure of.

Violet saw me through my worst moments. I'm not proud of the way I sometimes treated her during the year I was sidelined. I wasn't in my right mind at that time. She tolerated a lot from me. I think she felt sorry about my situation. She saw someone she loved publicly humiliated daily. For Violet, who had a huge heart, this was difficult to deal with.

At the time, my team had negotiated with the IAAF an acceptable testosterone level of no more than 10 nanomoles per liter (nmol/L). (This was a measure of how much of the hormone was present in my blood at a given time.) My blood would be regularly tested by the IAAF, and these blood draws always took place through surprise visits. One even happened on Christmas Eve, while I was having dinner with Violet.

Slowly, steadily, the tests began to show that the pills were working.

I decided that even though I was feeling sick, what mattered was that I was alive. I didn't know when I would run again, but I was going to be my old self, even if sometimes I felt like I was falling apart on the inside.

And then it finally happened. In June 2010, my testosterone levels had fallen enough that the IAAF officially freed me. I remember Greg came to the HPC to tell me in person. I smiled so hard my cheeks hurt. All I had to do was continue taking the pills. Continue poisoning myself.

CHAPTER SIXTEEN

THE COMEBACK

I WAS CLEARED TO RUN. MY FIRST RACE WAS ON July 15, 2010, in Lappeenranta, Finland. I won. 2:04:22. The second race was at the Savo Games in Lapinlahti, Finland, and there I won in 2:02:41. Far off from where I used to be, and I cannot say I enjoyed myself or that I was even fully there emotionally. The medication had already begun to destroy my system, and one day I was fine and the next day I felt terrible. I knew I still had speed but I didn't have access to my kick in the same way as before. I had to learn to strategize, control myself, learn to win from the front or the back, learn how to get out if I got caught in the middle.

But just being on the track kept me motivated. I was a competitor again. Life made sense again.

The media continued to speculate about me and my "condition." I resolved to not speak about it. If the media tried to bring it up, I would refer to the time I had been sidelined as being "difficult," and that was it.

By now I had turned nineteen. I had to walk back out into the world with this thing hanging around my neck. I wasn't oblivious to the stares and whispers from other runners. I just refused to bow. It is what it is, I would think to myself, you won't shame me off the track.

During the year I was exiled, while the whole world discussed my sexuality, my genitals, and my body's structure, I decided to turn inward, to love and know myself. I found myself, found my strength. I like to think I spent that time closing the channels of my weaknesses, as if they'd never existed. I had to be strong if I was going to survive this. I had to mute the world and the chatter. I didn't have to talk about anything if they had already put everything out there. People kept talking. I couldn't stop them from talking.

All I needed to do was be myself, contain myself, wait for the right moment, and then explode on the track. Let my running do the talking.

At the end of August, I returned to Berlin for the Internationales Stadionfest meet held on August 22, 2010, at the same stadium, almost a year to the day since I'd won the world championships. I knew there would be lots of media attention, but things would be different. I now knew things about life and the system that I hadn't known before.

Jukka and Michael had traveled with me, and they did

a great job of allowing only the journalists who respected my boundaries to speak with me. If a journalist cautiously referenced my yearlong absence, I would say "it wasn't easy to deal with" and then redirect the conversation to how happy I was to be back. And you can see it on my face during these interviews—my smile is wide and genuine.

When the gun went off, I remained patient. As the group of runners huddled closer, I was near the back of the pack. I wanted to get a feel for the pace and get comfortable. Once I had a good look around me, I settled in. A few runners passed me, and I pushed away the feeling of wanting to just go. Then I started to make a move around the 200-meter mark. Nothing crazy, just let my legs turn a little faster. I gave it all I had in the last 50 meters and slipped through an opening between the two leading runners. I crossed the finish line first with a time of 1:59:90. This was my first official sub-2 run in a year. Despite feeling heavy, I knew my heart, legs, and lungs still had it.

Fifty thousand people were at the stadium that day. I felt welcomed by the crowd, and I was glad I gave them a good show.

Right after the Berlin race, some of the other athletes showed their disdain for me and expressed concern about whether it was *right* that I was allowed to run again, especially if I began breaking records.

I could only shake my head. What were they talking

about? Elite athletes weren't supposed to break records? Wasn't that the entire point of sports? The problem here was obvious—the other athletes didn't want the person who broke them to be me.

My next race was in Brussels on August 27. This would be my first Diamond League event, and it featured a world-class field. The runners went out quickly, and I couldn't make a move in time. I placed third with 1:59:65. But it was a sub-2. That's what mattered.

My next two meets would be in Italy. The first meet was at the Palio Città della Quercia in Rovereto on August 31. I finished seventh with a time of 2:07:16. There I was just tired. The travel and the intense training right before the race took my legs away. The medication also prevented me from recovering as I normally would.

Our next plan was to run in the Commonwealth Games in New Delhi, which would take place in October 2010, but a back injury kept me in Pretoria. It was nothing major, just muscle strain from training. It meant I got time to heal, train, and spend time with Violet.

My training eased up a little bit with my injury and the holiday break. I returned to the University of Pretoria in January 2011, energized from the time I spent with my family and ready for the running season, even though I struggled with the medication. By now I'd gained weight. You could see it on my face, on my body. The media commented that my face looked "rounded" and "softer" and that my body had become "curvier" and more "feminine." Some newspapers placed markers/outlines over the supposedly new hips and breasts I'd magically sprouted and speculated on what kind of treatments I may have been undergoing. It was ridiculous.

My first race that year was in February at a Yellow Pages series race. I won the 800, although I wasn't as fast as I'd hoped, with a time of 2:04:12. I ran a few more races in my country and then traveled to the United States in early June. It was my first time in America and I was to run at the Prefontaine Classic Diamond League meet in Eugene, Oregon. This time, I managed to go under 2:00 with a time of 1:58.

A few days after Oregon, I went to the Bislett Games in Oslo, Norway. I did not run as well as I could have in this race. I ran out of steam at the 200-meter mark, but I still won a bronze medal. All that mattered to me was that I was there. Each of these races would prepare me for my next and most important goal—defending my world title in Daegu, South Korea, that coming September.

CHAPTER SEVENTEEN
LOVE AND HAPPINESS

BY NOW I KNEW I WAS READY TO LEAVE THE HIGH-LEVEL
protection of the HPC. I wanted to live as I had before, in
regular housing right outside the school's grounds. I was
tired of feeling trapped. I was racing again, so there was no
need to hide from the media in the way I had needed to the
previous year. I'd gathered what I could of myself and felt
strong enough to handle them.

Back then Violet and I weren't in a fully committed
relationship. Violet was allowed to come see me at the HPC,
and she would spend the night sometimes, but everyone,
including my family, still believed she was my best friend.
No matter how far I traveled or how long I was gone, I
couldn't stop thinking about her. As soon as I returned
from Norway, I told Violet I wanted to be in an exclusive
relationship. I told her that I planned to move from the

HPC and that we could start with her committing to stay with me a few nights a week.

Violet was hesitant, and I understood why. The five-year age difference between us bothered her, as did the fact that she had never had these kinds of feelings for another woman. I have always known I wanted to be with women only, and the age difference didn't matter to me. I loved and trusted her.

I don't know how the rumors started. What I do remember is that a man who worked with Kobus van der Walt, who was then the director of sport at the University of Pretoria, requested a meeting with me to ask me to begin dressing more femininely and to discourage my relationship with Violet.

Violet and me outside University of Pretoria's campus.

"We cannot have this kind of thing at the school because it doesn't look good."

I was offended. "Is this about clothes or my personal life? Either way, what do my clothes or my personal life have to do with my running? I'm here to run. Do people wear dresses on the track? And why are you bringing up my personal business?"

"Caster . . . I'm just a messenger here—" the man tried to continue, but I cut him off. I wasn't having this nonsense.

"Who I eat with, what clothes I wear, that's none of anyone's business. I came to this university wearing these clothes, and I came here to study and to win medals for the program and for my country. I am not your daughter. I am nothing to you."

My tone was harsh, and the guy was angry, but now he knew where I stood and could go tell everyone else.

But it wasn't long before the issue came up again.

I had always felt like everyone knew and understood me at the school. I'd been there for two years and no one had ever discussed my clothing or my personal life, at least not to my face. What I had been given at the University of Pretoria was a proper structure, a great support system. I felt accepted. I had never been judged or harassed here. But now, as I returned to running competitively, I was being asked to change.

After Berlin, it was hard for me to trust people, and

the conversation about my clothes and the rumors going around about Violet put me on edge. I place trust in certain people almost immediately because my mind tells me they deserve it. But people are human. Once that trust is broken, for me, it's over. It can never be repaired.

The beginning of the end of my relationship with Michael Seme happened when he chose to betray my trust and interfere in my personal life. He was one of the best coaches I have ever had, but in 2011 Violet told me Michael had pulled her aside and said the other runners in the group were uncomfortable with the way she and I were communicating. He'd heard there was something "not right" between us. He said if this were so, she was too old to be involved with someone my age. He told her that it seemed as if she was controlling me, taking advantage of my situation, and that maybe she was the one "teaching" me about things I shouldn't be doing.

Seme helped me become a great athlete, but he was not entitled to my feelings. He was an old-school Zulu man; they had their own beliefs about same-sex relationships. Even if I had a deep affection for him, at the end of the day I was an athlete. I never once cared or thought about Seme's personal life—he should not have interfered in mine.

I went straight to Michael and told him what Violet had said. Michael didn't deny it, and he told me he had done it for my own good. He said I had to concentrate on defending my title at the upcoming world championships, not on Violet.

"Let this thing with this woman go, Caster."

I was firm. "My relationship has not gotten in the way of my work for you. We are all making money. I am who I am."

I walked away from Seme. We both knew there was no coming back from this.

I went back to my room at the HPC and decided to call my father. Seme had threatened to call him and tell him about me and Violet, and I wanted him to hear it from his daughter, not her coach.

2011. I was running the last 10 kilometers of the Soweto Marathon. Violet came to support me.

"Dad. Look, Violet and I are in a relationship. We are more than friends. We have been for a long time. It's my personal business and it does not get in the way of my running. And I will not allow anyone to interfere."

This might be what Americans call "coming out of the closet," but I didn't see it that way. My family had always known where I stood; now they would just know who I stood with.

My father didn't sound surprised. He reminded us that we were Christians and that God told us not to judge. He added, "As your parent, Caster, all I want is for you to be happy. For you to be safe. You have been through a lot. That is all that matters to me."

Then we agreed I would come home so we could all talk as a family. I went home a few days later.

I remember my mother did not speak; she simply listened as the words spilled out of me.

"And I don't care about what other family thinks about this. Uncles, aunts—who are these people anyway? They have their own yards. Their own kids to worry about. I want to know where you stand, in this household, the household that matters to me. Because I don't want to hear from other people that you don't accept me. If you have a problem with me or with Violet, then I will no longer come stay in a place where I am not welcome."

I told them if it was difficult for them to live with me

such as I was, then I would leave the country, I would start my life all over again somewhere else. That's how much I loved Violet. How much I wanted to be with her.

When I was finished, my mother said, "Mokgadi. We know who you are. You have been good to us and you are blessed. What makes you happy makes us happy. Who are we to question other people's relations? This will always be your home."

My parents were not worldly people, but they knew my romantic life was a concern and an issue for many. At least South Africa's government had moved the country's thinking forward in terms of policy. To this day, South Africa is the only African country to have formally legalized same-sex marriage. This happened in 2006, the year Violet and I first met, when she mistook me for a boy in the women's locker room.

I hoped soon I would be able to take advantage of that freedom.

The South African national team traveled to South Korea in late August 2011. The field was competitive—Kenya's Jepkosgei would be there, as would Russia's Mariya Savinova and America's Alysia Montaño.

That 800-meter final was crazy. The pace was insane from the beginning. I thought I had it on the straightaway but somehow Savinova ran me down in the last 75 meters or so. When she flew by me, I knew it was over. She took the life out of my legs.

Savinova got to the line in 1:55:89. I was dying right behind her and got the silver in 1:56:35.

It was the first time in my life that I felt like I truly got hit by another runner. I respected her for that win. I still do, even after she was later stripped of her championship and Olympic medals for doping.

I didn't defend my world championship, but I had a silver medal. I was satisfied with my performance. Mariya—a runner who'd told the camera to "just look" at me in 2009—gave me a warm hug. Jepkosgei, who'd earned a bronze, made it a three-way hug. But when I went to congratulate the American, Alysia Montaño, she ignored me. I always say I'm not bothered by these things. The truth is this one stung. Alysia is African American. I considered her an ancestral sister.

But I walked away from Daegu feeling even stronger. More capable. Now I had to get back to my country and walk away from the people and, eventually, the place that had become a second home to me.

CHAPTER EIGHTEEN
ROAD TO LONDON 2012

SEME WAS SURPRISED WHEN I TOLD HIM I WAS LEAVING the group. I appreciated everything he'd done for me in bringing me to the university, but I did not owe him my heart or my body. Those were mine.

I would still run for the university's system, but I would no longer live inside school grounds. Now I was ready to face the world in a different way. Toby and David and everyone else at the school did well in taking care of me. But I wasn't a child anymore. I was a woman. I needed to be independent.

But I also wanted a coach. And fate would have it that one of the best 800-meter runners in history was living in South Africa.

If there ever was a runner I wanted to be like, it was

Maria Mutola. She was a powerfully built middle-distance runner who had dominated the 800-meter distance for over two decades, winning an Olympic gold and multiple world championships. She was a fellow African, from a small village in Mozambique. We had an almost twenty-year age difference, and she'd retired by the time I got to the elite level.

There had been rumors about her gender, too, but that's where they have stayed—as rumors. As far as the world knows, Maria had not been subjected to anything close to what had happened to me. But people did talk about her looks, the shape of her body. Sports insiders and those who ran against her would often comment that she wasn't feminine enough, that she wasn't "pretty" in whatever way women were supposed to be while still being able to run faster than most humans ever could.

I needed to be pushed in a different way. I wanted to work with someone who understood the physical pain of training, someone who had been a runner, someone who could demonstrate techniques. Seme was a great coach, but he was an old man set in his ways. Maria would understand that sexuality does not interfere with performance.

She and I began training at the end of 2011. The ultimate goal was the 2012 Olympics.

I didn't tell Maria I was on the medication. We had

traveled to Düsseldorf, Germany, for a couple of races, and my performances were so up and down that Maria didn't understand what was going on. She knew I was capable of going under 1:55, but since we'd begun working together, I hadn't even gone sub-2. I'd have a great first lap and then blow the second one. Nothing made sense to her.

After another terrible run in Germany, I finally came clean. "Maria, I have to tell you. They are making me take these drugs. I can't run without them. We're not going to get the results we wanted from this program, and you deserve to know because we are working hard but maybe this thing is not going to happen."

Maria did something I wasn't expecting. She started crying. Big tears came down her face right there as we both stood on the track. Seeing this strong woman cry broke my heart.

"This will not be an easy road, Caster. You may never achieve these dreams of yours. I am sorry for you. I am sorry this is how it has to be."

Perhaps a different coach would have left me, but Maria stayed. Her coaching style was brutal. She accepted nothing less than perfection and consistency. I had to follow her program. She pushed me to my limit, and despite the drugs, the extra weight, and generally feeling unwell, I qualified for the July 2012 London Olympics at the trials in Pretoria with a 1:59:58. It was the first time I'd gone sub-2 on South African soil.

Maria traveled with me to London. And so did my parents—after all these years of watching me on a television screen, my parents boarded an airplane for the first time and traveled overseas. I also had the great honor of being chosen as South Africa's flag bearer at the opening ceremonies.

Unfortunately, I knew even before I got to London that something was wrong. I couldn't feel my body. I did my job and made it through to the final, but I felt dead.

The lineup would be stacked with pure speed—Kenya's Janeth Jepkosgei and Pamela Jelimo, America's Alysia Montaño, an exciting nineteen-year-old Burundian named Francine Niyonsaba, who had already beaten me in prior races, and three Russians.

When the warm-up time came for the final run, I went over to my coach.

"Maria, I can't do it. I'm tired. I don't think I can run this thing."

Maria wouldn't hear of it. She just looked at me and said, "You'll be fine. Just do your thing." And with that she walked away from me toward her seat in the stands.

I went back to the track. Here is where I usually work out any nerves, I come into myself, I do my drills. This is where usually the other runners watch me and take themselves

My mom and dad in London 2012. They went on a tour of the
city. I also took them around the Olympic Village.

out of the race. Instead, I stretched and . . . fell asleep. On the field. At the Olympics. The place I'd dreamt of being since I started running.

"Semenya! Semenya! Come on, girl. It's time. SEMENYA!" It was the great Kenyan Janeth Jepkosgei, shaking me awake.

"What?! What?!" For a moment I had no idea where I was. I didn't even remember falling asleep.

Jepkosgei shook her head and looked at me like I was crazy. I turned over and grabbed my spikes. I tried to pull myself together. Whatever is going on, I don't know, but we will see, I thought.

We got to the line. I couldn't quiet my mind. The gun went off. I was in the back of the pack. Fighting for my life. You could see the strain and disbelief on my face. I remember thinking, What am I doing here?

I looked in front of me. Jelimo, Savinova, Jepkosgei . . . everybody was up there. I couldn't focus. My normally quiet mind wasn't quiet at all. Talking. Chattering to myself. I was moving, but nothing was flowing. When the bell rang for the final lap, I thought, This is over. I was dead last, with Niyonsaba right in front of me. I just couldn't gain speed. I have never admitted this publicly, but when I heard the bell signaling the halfway mark, I was about to jump out.

I have never quit a race in my life.

Starting out in the heats of the women's 800 meter.

Maria told me she'd been so saddened by the sight of me dragging on the track, she started to leave the stadium. She couldn't bear to watch what she knew was going to happen. And then she heard a collective gasp.

At 300 meters to go, I felt something in my body. Savinova was gone. Way out. No way to run that woman down, but something in me just kept saying, *One step at a time, Semenya. One step at a time, girl.*

I passed Niyonsaba and Montaño and some others. I thought about my mother and father in the stands, watching their child. They'd traveled to the other side of the world to see me. I could not jump out in front of my parents. My country had chosen me as the flag bearer. My people, my journey ... all those who'd supported me ... there was no way ... I had to keep going. Something reconnected between my mind and my body, some energy began to flow. I remember I started to really move. 200 meters. 150 meters. I passed more bodies. I'm looking. I'm looking and thinking, *There has to be a way to get up there ... keep going, girl, there's a bronze right over there. Get there and you're on the podium. OK ... we're at the straightaway now, girl. Let's hit it.*

And then I ran like I've never run in my life.

When I got through the line, I had won the Olympic silver medal in 1:57:23.

I would continue training with Maria and prepare for the 2013 season. Unfortunately, things went wrong almost right away. A week after we returned from London, during speedwork training at the university, I felt a click in my right knee. The same leg and injury that had put me in a hospital when I was seven.

"Does it hurt? If it doesn't hurt, finish the workout." Maria had the stopwatch in her hand.

I knew I shouldn't have, but I kept going. And by the time I finished, my knee had blown up to three times its size. Maria's eyes popped out of her head.

My first thought was how my private gynecologist had said I needed to retire right after I went to the Olympics. I hadn't listened to her. And now my leg was shot. I knew my season was over.

Maria couldn't believe it. She was an excellent coach, exactly what I needed to get where I wanted to be at that time, but sometimes the mistake athletes-turned-coaches make is treating the athletes they're training as if they are an extension of themselves. Maria only wanted to implement what had worked for her on me. And, like I said, Maria was a beast. We were similar athletes, but we weren't the same. Maria was about perfection, hitting whatever the plan was for that day, no matter what. That had worked for her. I was more intuitive when it came to workouts.

I went to SASCOC, the South African Sports Confederation and Olympic Committee, and told them I'd hurt my knee. They assured me I would continue to receive funding and that they were proud I'd brought home the silver medal. Yet in May 2013, while I was recovering, they removed me from their program, and I would no longer get paid.

I didn't see it coming. I'd brought them an Olympic silver medal and had injured myself. They'd said I had their support and then they abandoned me after just a few months. I remember thinking, OK. So this is how it works. SASCOC is not to be trusted.

The years 2013 and 2014 were the two worst of my running career. Despite physio and rehab therapies, my leg constantly bothered me. I could run through the pain and discomfort, but my times were terrible.

Then I lost my coach. Maria had to return to Mozambique to handle some financial affairs.

My training did not progress well enough for me to qualify for the August 2013 world championships in Moscow. I continued trying. On September 7, I managed to dip under 2 at the World Challenge meet in Rieti, Italy. I was feeling so ill that I don't know how I managed a 1:58:92.

By then it wasn't just my leg that was holding me back.

My theory is that my intense training regimen helped lessen the side effects of the drugs. Once I was injured and couldn't push myself in the same way, the side effects became worse.

By mid-2014, I realized I couldn't even run a 2-minute 800 meters, much less dip under it. I could not make a team.

It was hard for Violet to watch me suffer. One day I came home from training and went straight to our couch. I held my head in my hands.

"Caster?" Violet came over and sat next to me. I took a deep breath.

"I'm done, Violet. I'm not going to do this anymore. I need a break."

"A break? The Caster I know needs a break?"

I know Violet was trying to encourage me in this moment, to remind me of my fighting spirit. But I was done. Sometimes the right thing is to just sit still.

"I can't finish out the season." Once I said this out loud, all I felt was relief.

My last 800-meter race was the World Challenge meet in Madrid on July 19, 2014. I came in last of eleven runners, time 2:06.

This period of my life taught me a lot. Sometimes

quitting is the right thing to do. There are times when "powering through" really does more harm than good.

I returned to Pretoria and spent the winter at home, weighing my options. I was no longer running for the University of Pretoria. I remember Toby and I had a long talk. He'd always done right by me, but he agreed it was time for me to fly. Every bird has to leave the nest. He said I would always be welcome at the school, and he'd cleared things so I was authorized to train on their grounds.

Now I was free—completely independent. I spent my days resting, recovering, eating. Yet I felt sick the whole time. I gained even more weight. Time seemed to be all I had.

I was feeling so ill that I went to see my gynecologist. She ran some tests and the news was not good. The drugs were causing my twenty-three-year-old body to behave like I was a middle-aged menopausal woman. The hot flashes, night sweats, panic attacks, sleeplessness, and loss of concentration were getting worse. She reminded me the medication could also be weakening my bones, making me more prone to injuries.

"You were only supposed to do this for four years, Caster. That was it. I am telling you as a medical professional. You will continue to deteriorate."

I was stubborn. I told her I was going to keep running. I would know when it was time to end it. I was physically and mentally breaking down, but I refused to give up. There is a way back, I thought, even as I just lay around the house unable to do much of anything.

Violet came home from work one day and said some words that hurt me deeply but that needed to be said. Violet was one of those people whose soft demeanor and quiet voice could give people the wrong impression. Her kindness was not a weakness. She always told me the truth, even when I didn't want to hear it.

"I never thought I'd see you, Caster, behaving like a person who is done with life. You're just like all those people out there with no drive, no ambition. I told you a long time ago this running is not everything. It will be over one day. You know that. And now all you do is sit. You don't have an education. You never finished your degree. Where are you going to work? Who will hire you? Let me tell you this . . . I will not share my life with a person who had opportunities and just threw them away."

I will never forget Violet's face as she said these things. She was sad and furious with me. She was right. I had no drive. I wasn't me anymore. If I didn't at least get a diploma, how could I motivate other girls and women?

Here, I must say, I cried. I cried like a child. Those tears were hot. I felt pure shame. I thought of my parents. How hard they'd worked to make sure my siblings and I ate and had decent shelter over our heads. Everything they'd sacrificed just so that we could continue to draw breath on this earth. They'd never had a chance to get an education. I was better than this.

The first thing I did was get off the couch. Then I enrolled in a sports management program with the University of South Africa. It was a short course, but at least it was a start and I needed to reactivate my brains, to get back into the rhythm of being a student.

And I wasn't done with running. I was still an athlete, and I wanted to give it one more chance. I just needed a new environment, a new coach.

Around September 2014, I decided to call Jean Verster. He was a South African coach who had studied in the United States and had been an elite middle-distance runner in his day. He was known as one of the best coaches in the country and was now working at North-West University (NWU) in Potchefstroom, a city in South Africa's North-West province.

"Why, Caster," he laughed when he heard me introduce myself, "what a pleasure and a surprise." He sounded happy to hear from me and I got straight to the point.

"I would like to train with you. I don't think my career is over. I want to learn and I want to run. I still have it. I just need a place where I can find it again."

Jean told me that he'd admired my career and that he knew I'd been having some troubles. He said I'd done the right thing canceling my season, that my body was telling me to rest and I had to listen to it. Jean asked me to meet with the head of the NWU sports program the following week to see how we could work together.

When I did, the director offered me a three-year scholarship. I would study sports science.

Potch was about 180 kilometers away from Pretoria. Violet wasn't happy about the distance, but I would no longer be sitting. I moved to Potch in late October 2014. It was exactly what I needed—small and rural, almost like my own birth village. There were no distractions there—not much else to do but eat, study, train, and sleep, which is all I wanted.

Jean was a soft-spoken and deliberate man. He had a calming presence. He did not push me. What we needed, he said, was to get me back to basics. More than anything, Jean wanted me to rediscover my love of running. If he knew I was on the IAAF's drug regimen, he didn't let on. We never discussed it.

I trained and studied sports science with a passion I didn't know I could have. I also continued to take the poison. Jean and I created a beautiful relationship; we trusted each other, and I was slowly starting to climb back up mentally and physically. I allowed a few media interviews. I told myself to be happy, to stay positive, to salvage the feeling of hope I'd begun to have while there. I was determined to go to the Olympics in 2016, and I wanted another world championship.

On August 1, 2015, I surprised myself by qualifying for the Beijing world championship with a 2:00 800 meter at the trials in Linz, Austria. I wasn't feeling well and I still didn't have my form, but I would be back on the world stage after more than two years. The Beijing world championship would be taking place at the end of August, which meant I only had around three weeks to train.

I remember I was still packing my things in Austria to return home when I received a call from Greg.

"Hey Caster! How are you, my dear? How are things? How is the leg?"

I was glad to hear Greg's voice. Throughout the years, he'd never given up on me. By then we were more like father and daughter than lawyer and client.

"Greg, my man. I'm good. I'm happy. I just qualified for Beijing. I'm figuring things out but I'm feeling better."

"Well, I have news that will make you feel even better, Caster," Greg said. "The IAAF just lost a case about their testosterone regulations. You can stop taking the medication immediately. As of today. Right this second. They have two years to come up with scientific evidence that testosterone gives women an unfair advantage. You're free now, Caster."

I could hear the overwhelming emotion in his voice. Greg was so happy for me.

I don't remember, but I may have said something like, "OK, Greg. Thank you. I'll call you when I get back home." And I hung up. I didn't really know what to think. I wasn't sure I'd heard him correctly. I didn't get excited. I had lost the ability to be excited about things at that point in my life. I don't think I believed what I'd just heard. But then my phone rang again.

The next call was from Jukka, my manager.

"Caster, dear girl, did you hear? Did you hear about what's happened? . . . The IAAF dropped the regulations. HAHA!!! My girl . . . you know what this means, eh?" I could imagine Jukka's smiling face, his hands probably waving around excitedly.

"Hey . . . Yes. Thanks, Jukka. I heard something about this today, but . . . I don't know . . ." This news was hard to process. Like you are drowning and see someone coming to save you, but you don't know if they are real.

"Caster. Listen to me, it's real. You don't have to take the medication anymore. Now, my girl, you know what to do!" I can still hear Jukka's laugh when he said this. I couldn't help but laugh a little, too.

I stopped taking the medication that day. I threw the pills I had with me in the trash, and I felt the first stirrings of hope in my chest.

CHAPTER NINETEEN
GOLD IN RIO

2015 AND 2016 WERE YEARS OF RENEWAL. I REBUILT myself at Potch with Verster and his athletes. I had a single-minded focus and complete and total determination. I was going to be a champion again. I was going to find my way to the Olympics again. I was going to win gold medals. That was it.

My plan was to heal my body and mind. I drank as much water and electrolytes as my body could take and I sweated and peed like nobody's business. The pause in regulations seemed real, and I wanted to flush out as much of the poison as possible as quickly as I could.

I traveled to the world championships in Beijing in August 2015. This time, Jukka and Masilo from Nike traveled with me. It felt great to be back among top athletes, but after the first heat on August 26, I knew I wasn't going to make it to the final. I managed a 1:59:59, which qualified me for the 2016 Rio Olympics, but I went back to my room and just collapsed on the bed. The semifinals were the next day. I did not sleep well, and I didn't wake up feeling any better. As soon as I got to the stadium, I told both Jukka and Masilo I wasn't going to make it. The other women were just too fast, and my body was tired.

Masilo just put his arm around my shoulder and said, "You are fine, Mokgadi. Just go out there and give it what you can. Don't worry. Just be you."

I remember I lined up and the gun went off and I came in last with a time of 2:03:18. I dug deep for that run . . . I don't even know how I was able to walk back to the locker room. It was all I had. I can't say I was disappointed. You can never be disappointed when you know you gave everything.

I sat in Jean Verster's office after Beijing to have a conversation about my progress, what I wanted, what I believed I needed. Jean was not one of those "it's my way or there's the door" kind of coaches. He allowed me to combine everything I'd learned from Seme and Maria and create my own program, what I felt would work for me.

But Verster was different from them. He believed in gut feelings. Before every session, he would ask me how I felt that day. And I could be honest with him. If I said, "I don't feel like training hard today," he would honor that. What he wanted was to see me regain the joy of running.

And I was doing it. I could feel it coming back to me.

I took everything I'd learned until that point and combined it with Jean's program. I'd been studying anatomy, physiology, even psychology. The more I learned at Potch, the more I saw what had been missing with Michael and Maria and where I needed to add. At this point I had been on the drugs since 2009. For more than six years, the majority of my professional life, I had been running in a body that wasn't my own. This time, things would be different.

"Jean, I love you," I told him after a while. "I love your coaching style. But I think I must do this on my own. I need to focus on myself. You can focus on the other athletes. I don't want you to worry about me. I have to worry about me, and I have to worry about this leg."

Jean sat there in his office and listened. Even if he didn't agree with certain things, he was going to let me be me. Finally, he smiled.

"Do it, Caster."

My other focus was my home life. I had officially moved to Potch full-time in October 2015, but I was going back to Pretoria every weekend so I could spend time with Violet.

Violet and I knew we were going to spend our lives

together and had decided we were going to do it the right way. It was important to us that we honor our customs, our ancestors, in the way our families had been doing for generations. We planned to marry at the end of the year.

Violet and I are from the same tribe, but she was raised by a Tsonga family. The wedding customs are similar regardless of which tribe you're born into. I first consulted with my ancestors. I visited their graves, I prayed for guidance, and hoped for their blessing. I remember my grandfather came to me in a dream soon after. He told me the Semenyas were happy with my choice and would accept Violet into the family. Once I had this confirmation, I sat with my parents and my siblings and told them I wanted to marry Violet, and that I'd had our ancestors' blessing. My family was happy.

Now the process would begin.

My family first sent a letter to Violet's home. It essentially said the Semenyas had seen a rose in their yard, and we wanted to bring it home with us and nurture it there. Violet's family sent a letter back saying they had received our letter of intent and would like to hear more. This is how the negotiation for *lobola* begins. The *lobola* is a practical and respectful exchange of resources that cements a lifelong union between two families. And families don't just exchange money—it could be cattle, household items, or clothing.

These negotiations can feel almost like a game of chess; and even if you know the outcome, it can still be very suspenseful. Only the elders and family representatives may speak. If the families are not seeing eye to eye, there is usually a big show of walking away and trying again another day. Thankfully, we came to an agreement that same day. I had brought everything with me, and then the fun began.

We spent hours singing and dancing and eating. Violet came back with us to my birth village at the end of the festivities, and she spent the weekend at my parents' home fulfilling the customary duties of a new daughter-in-law. We were officially married in the eyes of our tribal law.

My life was good. I felt blessed. In 2015, I had a coach I trusted and a system where I was allowed to be myself; my body was coming back to me, and now I was a happily married woman.

The South African National Championships were to be held in Stellenbosch in April 2016. I told Jean that he should sign me up for three races—I was going to run the 400-, 800-, and 1,500-meter events. He thought I was insane. "You can't do that, Caster." I did it. I became the first woman, the first human, to run and win all three races in a four-hour time span. Soon after, I traveled to the African championships in Durban (a city in South

Africa) on June 26. I won the gold in the 800 meter and 1,500 meter, and anchored the winning team in the 4 × 400 meter relay.

I remember I didn't like the way my ankle felt after the relay. I limped a little when I was going to get my medals, but it was nothing to worry about. When the races were over, an ASA official asked if I would greet the new president of the IAAF, a man named Sebastian Coe. I don't remember specifics; all I remember is a White man in a black suit. I said, "Nice to meet you, sir," shook his hand, and then told him I had somewhere I needed to rush off to.

I should have stayed home and rested after I came back from Durban, but I pushed on. My next big race was a Diamond League meet in Monaco on July 15. I wanted to make a fast time, make it clear to everyone I was back in form. And I set a new 800-meter national record there with a 1:55:33 run.

And then my ankle . . .

Violet came to pick me up at the airport, and I could barely walk. My ankle was huge, as big as a baby's head. I'd broken my navicular bone playing baseball when I was a teenager, and it had never healed properly. I knew I'd aggravated the same injury. We were one month away from the Olympics.

I had several MRI scans done in South Africa, and Jukka sent them to Dr. Hans-Wilhelm Müller-Wohlfahrt in Germany, a famous orthopedist known for helping elite athletes get back on their feet. He called and said that in his expert opinion I was out of the Olympics. It was a stress fracture.

"This girl will not run," he'd told Jukka.

When Jukka called me with the news, I said, "Respectfully, Jukka, he doesn't know me." I refused to accept or even entertain the idea that I would miss the Olympics. I had a chance to win a gold medal. Not silver, not bronze. Gold. And that medal was mine.

My thinking was that if I was going to break my ankle for good, if I never ran again after the 2016 Olympics, then let it be so. After everything I'd been through, for me, it was an Olympic gold medal now or never.

I didn't want it to get out that I was injured. Competitors smell blood in the water when they find out about these things. I asked Jean to please not alert any of the school officials. I would do my best to walk normally whenever I came across people at the school or on the street. It was easy because I had a distinct limp from my knee injury when I walked anyway. The moment I was out of their sight, I would have to stop myself from screaming in pain.

My favorite physiotherapist, Anita van der Lingen, was incredibly talented, and she tried her best, but she could not bring the swelling down. I realized there are times Western medicine is fine, and there are times when we need to do things in the way of our ancestors. So, just like I'd seen my grandmother do for those she treated, I grabbed a razor and cut myself to let out the bad blood.

The swelling came down, and Anita was shocked when she saw me again. We kept working on the ankle, and about two or three weeks before the Olympics, we heard a click. My ankle wasn't back to normal, and it still hurt, but something had snapped back into place. We began strapping the ankle while I continued to train, mostly in the gym. I went out to the track and realized I could now run straight, but I couldn't run the bends. I made the decision to do only the straightaway and attempt the bends once I got to Rio.

I'd hoped to run in the 400 and the 800 meter, but given the state of my leg, it was best to just keep it to the 800 meter.

"You will have to trust me, Coach," I told Verster the night before the race. "You just have to trust me because I am trusting my body."

By now everyone knew that IAAF's loss in court meant that I, along with anyone else suspected of having a DSD, would be running free. It seemed that everyone was talking about it on television, the radio, social media.

My win in the 800 meter seemed "inevitable" not because I'd been training and running well, but because people felt I had something that made my winning unfair.

Yet they thought nothing of cheering on the seeming inevitability of wins by genetically gifted athletes like Usain Bolt, who boasted millions more fast-twitch muscle fibers and a stride that was several inches longer than his peers. No one suggested Michael Phelps's dominance was unfair and he should have surgery to fix his hypermobile joints. Swimmer Katie Ledecky was never accused of being a man because she smashed multiple world records, and her ever-improving times in several events would actually qualify her for the men's Olympic team. But it mattered if I won because I represented something abnormal.

Things got so crazy that Olympic officials feared I would be physically harmed, and they hired armed guards to protect me at the stadium. It didn't matter to me. I focused on training and getting used to the conditions. I tried to shut out as much of the noise as I could. The day before the opening ceremonies, new IAAF president Sebastian Coe stated they were surprised at the ruling by the Court of Arbitration for Sport (CAS) striking down the testosterone regulations. He told the media they would revisit the issue in the next year.

I felt stable, my system strong and healthy. I felt whole; physically better than I had in years, even though I arrived at the Maracaña Stadium with only one good leg. The only people who knew my ankle was a potential issue were Verster, Jukka, Violet, Masilo, and my physio, Anita.

Two hours before the 800-meter final run, Sebastian Coe made a second public statement vowing the IAAF would go back to CAS with the proper evidence and have their regulations reinstated. To me, it was just another bullying tactic. And it felt very, very personal.

Unfortunately, the chatter about the 800-meter final was brutal. Some of the other female athletes were busy getting in front of cameras and lamenting they would be running for "bronze," or anonymously giving quotes about how "unfair" the situation in the final was going to be.

I had long ago learned to use people's nonsense to fuel my performance. So I did my thing during the warm-ups. I made sure each athlete and their managers and coaches saw me. Whatever direction my competitors were coming from on that track, they would see me preparing and know I was there to conquer. I was there to win. I wanted what I had been dreaming of since I started this journey—an Olympic gold medal. I didn't really care then or now what they were talking about.

I remember I stood in lane three going over my plan in my head. It wasn't different from what I'd done in the past, but I had a different kind of determination this time. I was prepared for this to be the last race I'd ever run. My body and mind were fully connected. I was present and ready.

The gun fired, and off we went. No one broke out in front. After the first bend, my ankle was still good, and I settled in on the inside. I took the lead, but not by much. I didn't want to get ahead of myself.

Don't kick too early.

I couldn't see anything beyond the track in front of me, but I could hear the steady pounding of the other runners just behind me. I glanced quickly over my right shoulder and saw a runner named Francine Niyonsaba. She was quickly gaining pace. I stared straight ahead.

Run your race. Steady.

OK, Semenya, get ready for it, girl . . .

Fifteen more seconds and there was the bell for the final lap. Francine wanted to move to the inside, and she was running faster than I wanted to, so I let her pass. I didn't want to mess her up. No collisions. She was the leader now. But I didn't think the young girl could sustain her surge. I could hear her breathing. I resisted the urge to get in front of her again.

Hold yourself . . . wait for it . . .

I was just behind her, feeling comfortable where I was. My chest was high, my arms pumped rhythmically, I controlled my breaths and just let her carry me along. It was a good position. I knew she was the only person I needed to beat. The rest of the pack was now chasing us.

And then it was time. The straightaway. Pure speed now.

I planted my feet a little more firmly, asked my body for more, and it responded right away.

I was in the zone now, everywhere and nowhere at the same time. *You can get there, girl. Keep going. It's yours. That gold is yours.*

I am sure in the moment I thought of nothing. But now when I think back to that race, I feel that perhaps images would have come and gone in my mind.

Me running barefoot in the rain, my legs and feet caked with mud. I could see myself back in our yard caring for our animals.

Run like a madwoman. Let's go, girl . . .

I could see my mother and father in our village and how in this moment they would be sitting in front of the television, holding each other, hearts beating as one, screaming at this daughter of theirs to GO!

And my friend and now wife. How back in 2009 Violet had given me the South African flag to carry with me to Berlin. How she'd told me to get off my ass and get an education.

I was sprinting now. The last gear. After this, I would have nothing left. Now I could hear the crowd roaring. I knew I'd left Niyonsaba behind.

There it is, girl . . .

I saw the line. I crossed it.

I'd won the gold. 1:55:28. A new national record.

Niyonsaba came in second, and Margaret Wambui had

come out the winner in a hard-fought battle for bronze with Canada's Melissa Bishop.

Just like at the Beijing 2008 Olympics, this was a clean sweep for the continent of Africa. I was so proud of us in that moment.

Right after, I did the Cobra and went to congratulate the other runners. It had been a great race. There hadn't been any falls or jostling, and several of the women also set national records and personal bests.

Wambui, Niyonsaba, and I went straight to the winners' press conference after the race, and the first question asked

was about our gender and whether the IAAF had made all of us take hormone treatments and what effect it had on our running.

I was tired. Just tired of all of this. I'd dealt with it for almost a decade. I'd swallowed my poison. I had suffered enough, and I could see in that moment how my suffering would be passed on to a whole new generation of young girls who'd done nothing but work hard and left it all on the track. Like me, they would run their hearts out and be reduced to their genitals and whatever biological issue others thought they had.

"Excuse me, my friend," I said to the journalist, "we are not here for that. Ask questions about the race. Don't ask us about the IAAF. Ask us how it went, how we're feeling. Ask us about our performance. This press conference is all about the 800 meters that we ran today. That's it. That's what matters." The room went silent. I sucked the air out of it.

With that, I hoped I set the tone that people like Sebastian Coe and other IAAF officials should have.

I called my family as soon as I got back to my room. I never took the medal off. It was still around my neck when I got into bed. I remember I wrapped a blanket tightly around myself and held on to that gold medal as you would your own child. I remember running my fingers over the front of the medal, which featured Nike, the goddess of victory. The 2016 Olympic medals were huge. Bigger than the palm of a hand. Much bigger than the ones from London in 2012.

When I got back to South Africa the next day, I handed the gold medal to my Violet right then and there in front of everyone at OR Tambo International Airport. No one deserved it more than her.

THE COBRA

THROUGHOUT THE END OF 2017 AND INTO 2018, I continued to win medals, and I broke a national record in the 1,500 meter that had stood for over thirty years. I also graduated with a diploma in sports science from North-West University. I was now officially an educated woman.

Again and again, I won. But my fight was not over.

Perhaps it never will be.

Seb Coe had made it clear at the Rio Olympics that the IAAF would find a way to reinstate the testosterone regulations. So they commissioned another testosterone study by their own Dr. Stéphane Bermon. He was the same doctor who back in 2009 had told my team the IAAF's "preferred method" of dealing with women like me was a gonadectomy.

Their new study, which was published in May 2017,

compared natural testosterone levels of elite females and elite males in various events to come up with the results that women with higher testosterone outperformed other women. Prominent doctors, scientists, and academicians agreed the study was full of errors.

These scientific opinions did not matter to the IAAF, though. In April 2018, they announced their new testosterone regulations, which would apply to athletes with what they called "differences of sexual development" (DSD), and only to those competing in the 400-, 800-, and 1,500-meter distances.

My three events.

In these three races, the testosterone limit would be lowered from the original 10 nmol/L they'd announced in 2011 to 5 nmol/L for a period of six months before an affected athlete was eligible to compete. And it would need to stay at 5 nmol/L or below whether in or out of competition, even if an athlete was resting or injured.

The new rules would come into effect in November 2018. They were giving me seven months to comply.

For the next few months, I participated in as many major events as I was physically capable of—I traveled to Doha, Eugene, Oslo, Paris, Monaco, and Zurich. I continued to set national and track records. As the clock wound down, I understood the options: go back to poisoning myself but twice as hard, agree to irreversible, life-altering surgery and then spend the rest of my days taking pills anyway to regulate my body's hormones, change my events, or walk away from athletics.

I wasn't going to comply with the medication or have surgery. I was not ready to quit. But I realized I had another option.

Someone had to fight the IAAF.

It would not be easy, but I had no choice. I never backed down from bullies as a kid and I wasn't about to do so now.

In early June 2018, my team and I announced we would challenge the IAAF.

My case against the IAAF was scheduled to begin on February 25, 2019, at the Court of Arbitration for Sport in Lausanne, Switzerland. The court was supposed to be an independent body created to settle sports disputes between athletes and sports federations. The arguments would be about gender, medical ethics, and the very idea of "fairness" in sports.

Greg and I flew to Geneva. I remember that the night before the trial, I went for a run alone to clear my thoughts. I felt so far away from home. Violet was newly pregnant. We had been trying in vitro fertilization (IVF), a method of fertilizing an egg outside a woman's body, then placing it into her uterus, and it had worked. Yet now she was thousands of miles away.

I regained my calm. All I had to do the next day was tell the truth and let God handle the rest. Win or lose, it would be my opportunity to finally tell the world what I'd been through.

That morning, Greg and I walked through a crowd of media into the Château de Béthusy building. I held my head high and flashed the cameras a peace sign. Once inside, we were directed to a main room with a long rectangular wooden table surrounded by chairs. It was not a courtroom in the way most people imagine it. It gave you the sense of a roundtable discussion.

Our argument was that I was a woman, even with my body's differences, and that the rules were discriminatory because they only applied to women. Men didn't have to physically prove they were in the right category on account of some rumor. They didn't have a testosterone range they had to adhere to. We argued the rules were both physically and psychologically harmful to all women and that the regulations should be thrown out because they lacked scientific evidence proving my body's differences gave me any kind of "unfair" advantage in my sport.

The IAAF claimed it was a private organization, and that as such, they were not directly subject to human rights

Greg and me in Switzerland.

law. They could discriminate at will if they believed their regulations were a "necessary and proportionate" way of achieving a "legitimate objective."

The trial started with me introducing myself and my story. I didn't feel nervous. I felt determined. I told the panel where I came from, how I'd become an elite runner. I told them about the 2009 Berlin incident and how the way I was treated in front of the world continued to haunt me. I told them I agreed to take the drugs because at that time I was desperate to run, but that it had caused me great physical and mental anguish.

For a full week, I was cross-examined, called "a biological man," and accused of cheating. I listened to IAAF's experts say that I could have run faster, had manipulated my hormone levels, and that if I'd had surgery, it would have had no negative effects.

Not one of these experts looked me in the eye when they were speaking. But I looked at them, and I spoke honestly.

"The IAAF confiscated my life. They confiscated my rights as a human being. I was a child then. Look at what was done to me."

I heard the judges and lawyers and experts talking and arguing with each other. At some point it all just became noise to me. To me, this was a fight for my life, my identity, my livelihood.

When the proceedings were over, I knew things

wouldn't go in my favor. And they didn't. On May 1, 2019, the CAS agreed the rules were discriminatory, but said that they were reasonable enough for the IAAF to protect the female category. The panel agreed the science was not conclusive and suggested the IAAF take some more time to do research before implementing the regulations.

I knew the IAAF wouldn't waste any time. They imposed the new rules one week later.

I decided to travel to Doha to run in the Diamond League season opener on May 3. It would be the last race before the regulations went into effect. I won the 800 meter in 1:54:98. It was my thirtieth consecutive win in the 800-meter event, the fastest time of the year, and a meeting record.

On May 29, my team appealed the CAS verdict to the Swiss Supreme Court on the grounds that it was discriminatory, and I put out a public statement: "I am a woman and I am a world-class athlete. The IAAF will not drug me or stop me from being who I am."

This fight had gone beyond me proving I had no advantage on the field over other women. This fight was about human rights.

I ran my last IAAF-sanctioned 800-meter race on June 30, 2019. It was the Diamond League Prefontaine Classic in Stanford, California. I knew, even before I arrived, that it would be my last time running the 800 meter on an international stage. It was a forced retirement on this part of my career.

That day, I walked to the starting line. The last thing I remember thinking before I quieted my mind was, You will not lose this race.

When they announced my name to the crowd, I lifted my fist in a power salute. Then I won in 1:55:69, the fastest time on US soil, setting a new national record.

Violet's and my daughter was born in July. Life completely changed in that moment. I remember when I first held my daughter in my arms. I knew I would spend the rest of my days making sure she was safe and happy. I felt the same way when our second daughter was born in July 2021.

Becoming a parent changed my perspective and my priorities. I recognized that much of my life had been centered on myself and the single-minded pursuit of my talents. Even though I believe God has used me for a higher purpose on this earth, I had been completely and totally focused on performing and winning. I could no longer do those things. I was a mother now.

The more information that came out about the IAAF's

regulations and the fiction behind their research, the more support I received from women's groups, international and South African media, and female athletes who had weathered sexism, racism, and controversies over their looks, like Serena Williams, Billie Jean King, and so many others. Nike, the first company that believed in me, created a beautiful campaign about the resilience of women and celebrating and accepting our differences. I was also chosen as one of *Time* magazine's 100 Most Influential People.

I appreciated the love and support, and I did feel hopeful, although, as I've said, I am a practical girl.

Once I knew the Swiss court had closed the door on my favored events pending the outcome of the appeal, I discussed the future with my team. I wanted to go to the 2020 Tokyo Olympics, I wanted to defend my 800-meter title, but the reality was that the only way to compete was to move down to the 200 meter or up to the 5,000. That was a decision I would have to make almost immediately. It takes an athlete around two years to properly train their body for a specific event. And I was no longer a teenager. I was nearing the age of thirty. The body is an incredible gift, but it has its limits.

I began training for Tokyo in November 2019. There was a chance the Swiss court would overturn the regulations before the start of the Olympics, but I had to be prepared in case that didn't happen. Sometime in March, I publicly stated I would attempt the 200 meter in order to continue competing at the highest levels and hopefully get to the Olympics.

The Olympics were scheduled to be held in July 2020 but were postponed for a year because of the COVID-19 pandemic. This gave me clarity. I would move up in distance. I would attempt to qualify for the 5,000 meter. It was the right choice, given my age and physical condition. I needed to take care of myself, take care of my body, and prepare for longevity. I wasn't going to tear up my muscles to sprint—I'm a sports scientist; I know my body's limitations.

I began training in earnest for the 5,000 meter. I knew the Olympic qualifying time was around 15:10, and I wasn't anywhere near it. By April 2021, I was running the 5,000 in 15:52:28, and by May I had dropped the time down to 15:32:15. At the end of June, I traveled to Europe to see if I could qualify for the Olympics. I went to Belgium, Austria, Germany—but my body just didn't feel right. In all the qualifying races I tried, the first 3 kilometers would be fine but not great, and the last 2 kilometers would be just awful. My body was tired. I knew I was done and called off the season. There would be no Olympics for me. As they say, God gives and God takes away.

I returned to South Africa just in time for the birth of my second daughter, in July 2021.

On March 23, 2023, Seb Coe announced the IAAF had new regulations. It would still allow women with DSDs to compete, but they would now have to lower their testosterone from 5 nmol/L to 2.5 nmol/L or below for a continuous twenty-four months, whether training or resting, to compete in any discipline. For those currently running in the 400-, 800-, and 1,500-meter distances and taking the drugs under the regulations set in 2019, the IAAF lowered the time threshold to a continuous six months. This means none of these girls were able to compete in the 2023 Budapest world championships, nor would they be able to, most likely, in the 2024 Paris Olympics or the 2024 Glasgow world championships. Which was the point, of course. The IAAF also banned all transgendered athletes who had experienced puberty past the age of twelve across all disciplines.

For women like me, it was a complete ban under the guise of a new regulation. Seb Coe and the IAAF know that no human can maintain the same level of any hormone from one day to the next, even from sunup to sundown. The body doesn't work that way.

I will not take the drugs. So I will enter a different stage in my life now. I have my family and two degrees. I will always be a runner, IAAF or no IAAF. Violet and I have our youth program, the Masai Athletics Club, where we house and train young South African athletes. I will always be here, nurturing and protecting young talent. You may see me there on the track coaching the next world champion or Olympian, or simply sitting in the stands enjoying the show. The IAAF can't get rid of me.

I realize that every time I've experienced a great loss in my career, God and my ancestors have seen fit to give me something greater. That something is love. Even when I closed myself off to the world, when the nothingness has threatened to swallow me, I was given love—from my family, my wife, my friends, even strangers. I was given new life to love and foster in my daughters. I plan to do as much as I can with this life I was given. Whatever the future holds for me, I am not afraid; I know I am strong enough to carry it. In the end, I won the race that truly mattered.

I believe I'm a living testimony of God to show that when you are given life, never take it for granted. I was given a body, I was given a soul, I was given a brain, a heart, and all the organs in my body. I am using them each and every day. And I love being different, I love when I'm walking around and people think I'm a man and then realize I'm a woman. I'm present. I'm alive.

Some people have asked me if I ever just wished I'd

been born a man. Wouldn't it have been better for me? The thing is, I don't want to be a man. If my body's makeup makes me "intersex," as they say, then I'm intersex. There's nothing to be done about that. The terms will change as the years go by. They always do. To me, they're just words.

This story has many roads, some winding, others straight, some wide, others narrow—all led to my becoming Caster Semenya, the Daughter of South Africa. My story isn't about running so much as it is about what it means to be a human. In the beginning, I was just a runner. Today, I have become a symbol of resistance and freedom and self-acceptance. It's no longer about winning a race, it's about the struggle for universal human rights.

We have now taken the fight to the European Court of Human Rights. It has been given priority status. I hope there is a favorable outcome for the young girls who are now and will be subject to the regulations. I hope there is a favorable outcome for all women, for they will come to see that these regulations will affect them, too.

I will run as long as my body allows me to, and then I will walk away with my head held high, with my dignity intact. At the end of the day, I live for those I love, I live for the people who believe in the work I do. I mind my business, and I don't back down from any challenge. I stand strong, and I stay in control. I am Caster. I will always be myself. No one can rule over my life. That is what I call the Cobra mentality. That is the code I have lived and will continue to live by.

One day, this part of my life will be over. There will be no more speeches asked of me, no events I need to attend. Everyone will stop talking. All the noise will be silenced. It will just be me and mine. And when I think of that future, I think of myself back where I started. Back in the village of my birth.

I am Mokgadi Caster Semenya. Remember the meaning of my name—I am the one who gives up what they want so that others may have what they need. I am the one who seeks, I am the one who guides.

ACKNOWLEDGMENTS

There are many people to thank for this journey. I know it will seem like I have forgotten many of you. To those who have not been named, just know you are in my heart and mind, and that circumstances did not allow me the time and space to properly address you.

To my mother, father, and ancestors, I thank you for giving me life. It is a blessing to be on this earth and I will cherish every breath for the rest of my days.

To my siblings, cousins, and entire family, I thank you for loving and appreciating me just as I am. For never judging and criticizing me, for accepting the will of my life. Without your love and support, I would not be the person I am today.

To Violet, my wife and friend—my all—thank you for being there, for your patience, love, and constant care. For letting me be myself for you. You have understood me more than I understood myself. You are my soul mate. We ride together, we die together.

To Maseko, Ezekiel, Principal Perhaps, and many more during my early days as a runner: You all saw the potential for greatness in this little girl and allowed me to go out there and showcase my talent. You made sure I got to all the competitions I needed to be at. If it wasn't for these men, I wouldn't be here. I will never in my life forget it.

To the University of Pretoria, especially Toby Sutcliffe, Coach Michael, and my protector David—you opened the doors for this rural girl with dreams of living in the city. Thank you for showing me light, giving me guidance and protection. I would not have become a world champion without your support system. You will always remain in my heart.

To Greg Nott—may God bless you for coming to the aid of a little girl who just wanted to run. I am forever grateful for your continued love, kindness, patience, and understanding.

To all the lawyers, doctors, experts, and activists who rallied to my cause, who fight every day for universal human rights, I thank you from the bottom of my heart.

To everyone at the Tshwane University of Technology, especially Drs. Pen and Given, thank you for believing in me and helping me to achieve things academically I could never imagine. Thank you for pushing me and making a space for me in a place I didn't think I could fit into. The genuine love and time you continue to give me is priceless.

To North-West University, especially coach Jean Verster and athletics manager Terseus Liebenberg: I thank you from the bottom of my heart for the opportunity you gave me to find my inner peace, to reactivate and rebuild myself in body and mind. You saw I still had the potential for greatness, and I am happy I was able to deliver on the promise I made.

To my Nike family, especially Masilo—thank you for never giving up on me no matter what, thank you for accepting and celebrating me through the good and bad, thick and thin. I am eternally grateful for your time, effort, support, and patience throughout my career.

To my Wiphold family, you've been there since day one. I cannot thank you enough for protecting, appreciating, and accepting me for who I am.

To my Discovery family, I thank you for your unwavering support and unconditional love throughout this journey. It is a joy to work with all of you.

To Jukka, Masilo, Maria, and Becky—you have all played a massive role in my life and career. You have all made sure I achieved the best possible outcome in everything I did. Thank you for never judging or criticizing me and picking me up when I faced what seemed like insurmountable challenges. I am grateful for your presence in my life. May God bless you all.

To my physios, especially Anita van der Lingen—thank you for healing my body and helping me stay on the track. Thank you for the great work you've done to make sure my body is in shape, and that it always recovers well. Know that I appreciate the time you've sacrificed with your families to travel around the world with me.

To my strengthening coach, Jacus Coetzee—you are one in a million. You have helped me understand my body and helped me become the great athlete I am today. Because of you, I was able to discover the strength in me, what I could truly achieve. All you have wanted was for me to be great. Know that you are always in my thoughts.

To every pacer I've run with—thank you for doing a great job, for allowing me to explore the world with you, helping me run consistent times, getting me to where I needed to be. Without your work, no runner can reach their full potential.

To Peter McGuigan at Ultra Literary Agency, Norm Aladjem at Mainstay Entertainment, Tom Mayer and Nneoma Amadi-obi and everyone at W. W. Norton, Lemara Lindsay-Prince and all the Penguin Random House UK staff, Sibongile Machika and Annie Olivier and everyone at Jonathan Ball Publishers, and Sulay Hernandez at Unveiled Ink—thank you for allowing me to tell my story, for giving me this opportunity to connect with the world, and bringing the world closer to me so that I could be understood better not only as a great athlete but as a humble human being. Thank you all for your patience. I have truly enjoyed this experience and appreciated learning about the publishing business.

And finally, my eternal gratitude to the South African nation, for your unconditional love, support, and respect, despite my flaws and through my ups and downs. Thank you for celebrating my achievements and resilience in sports without judgment. Thank you for standing beside me, wrapping your arms around me, and lifting me up. May God bless you all.

With love,
Mogkadi Caster Semenya

PICTURE CREDITS